Hear Our Prayer

Prayers of the People for
the Revised Common Lectionary

by

Lisa Graves

&

Jon M. White

© 2024 by Lisa Graves and Jon M. White

All rights reserved.

Portions of this book may be reproduced by a congregation for its own use. Commercial or large-scale reproduction, or reproduction for sale, of any portion of this book or of the book as a whole, without the written permission of Church Publishing Incorporated is prohibited.

Typeset by Nord Compo
Cover design by Newgen

Library of Congress Cataloging-in-Publication Data

Names: Graves, Lisa, and White, Jon M - authors.
Title: Hear Our Prayer : Prayers of the People for the Revised Common Lectionary
Description: New York : Church Publishing, 2024.

Identifiers: LCCN 2024001913 | ISBN 9781640656949 (paperback) | ISBN 9781640656932 (epub)
Subjects: LCSH: Prayers. | Common lectionary (1992)
Classification: LCC BV245 .G638 2024 | DDC 264/.13—dc23/eng/20240308
LC record available at https://lccn.loc.gov/2024001913

Church Publishing
19 East 34th Street
New York, NY 10016

Table of Contents

Introduction   v

Principal Feasts & Holy Days   1
Lectionary Year A   23
Lectionary Year B   91
Lectionary Year C   159

Introduction

These prayers grew out of our podcast, the Subversive Undercroft. We wanted to share with others the good conversations we were already having about the role of the church in our lives and in our world, contemporary issues that the church faces, and just how compelling we found the words and example of Jesus.

Because we are both priests and inspired from the passage in First Thessalonians where the believers are encouraged to "pray without ceasing," we wanted to place our conversations within a structure that was prayerful and reverent while also fun and hopefully, informative, and inspiring. While our main focus was to talk about one of the readings from the Sunday lectionary each week, we also wanted to enter into prayer with our listeners, and so we conceived the idea that we would take turns writing "prayers of the people" for each episode.

Since that beginning, we have used these prayers in our congregations, editing, adjusting, and refining them to the point where we felt we wanted to share them with the wider church. As followers of Jesus, we have been deeply motivated by his vision of human life being centered around the idea of loving action.

We hope that these prayers reflect that desire for gospel action on the part of God's people and it is our truest desire that you might make these prayers your own.

This book offers prayers of the people intended to be used for congregational worship. The first section is prayers for the Principal Feasts and Holy Days from the calendar in the Book of Common Prayer (BCP).

The second section has prayers aligned with the proper for each Sunday of the 3-year Revised Common Lectionary. Our inspiration for these prayers comes from Form IV of the Book of Common Pray. Each set of prayers includes intercessions for the church, nation, and local community and follows the pattern and rubric of the Book of Common Prayer. The intercessions are for:

1. The universal Church
2. The nation and all in authority
3. The concerns of the local community
4. Those who suffer and those in any trouble
5. The welfare of the world
6. Those who have died

We have also included options for additional intercession which may be included from time to time or as contemporary events call for, including prayers from the Anglican Cycle of Prayer, a diocesan prayer cycle, and prayers for a companion diocese. As the prayers are those of the gathered community, it is recommended that a communal response be included. For simplicity's sake, each of the prayers includes the response, "Lord in your mercy, hear our prayer." You may wish to use a different response or none at all.

Some examples of other responses might be:

Hear us O God **and answer our prayer.**
God of (*Love, Wisdom, Mercy, Truth, Justice, etc.*), **hear our prayer.**
O Holy One, **hear our prayer.**

In the prayers intended for use in the principal weekly worship, we have also included optional wording for including a prayer list. Though some may worry about a prayer list becoming too long, we have found that many people find great comfort and courage sharing their prayer concerns with the whole assembly. Alternatively, rather than maintaining a list, the intercessor might say instead: "especially those you now name either silently or aloud" and then pause a moment while congregants offer up their own names.

If a prayer list is maintained, reasonable limits could be placed such using only first names, limiting the time names appear, or limiting the intercessions only for those facing acute health issues or other crises.

In many Episcopal Churches, it may also be the custom to pray for certain persons and relationships that are important to the local church, such as the diocesan and presiding bishops, churches of the Anglican Communion and other cycles of prayer, such as for parishes of the diocese or for congregations in a companion diocese with which the parish has a connection. It is our recommendation that these prayers be inserted after the first intercession and can be constructed as following:

We pray for the Church in (*Anglican Communion Province*) and for the whole Anglican Communion.
We pray for own church, for N. our Presiding Bishop, for N., our bishop(s) and for our whole diocese, especially *parish name, city*.
And we pray for our companion diocese of *name of diocese in relationship* [especially the parish of *N.*].
Lord in your mercy, **hear our prayer.**

Other intercessions of special concern to the congregation should be inserted prior to the intercessions for the dead. Below are some suggested intercessions that you may find helpful.

For A Birthday

Adapted from #50 page 830 of the Book of Common Prayer, 1979

O God, our times are in your hand: Look with favor, we pray, on your servant N. as *she* begins another year. Grant that *she* may grow in wisdom and grace, and strengthen *her*
trust in your goodness all the days of *her* life; through Jesus Christ our Lord. Amen.

Adapted from #51 page 830 of the Book of Common Prayer
Watch over your child, O Lord, as *her* days increase; bless and guide *her* wherever *she* may be. Strengthen *her* when *she* stands; comfort *her* when discouraged or sorrowful; raise
her up if *she* fall; and in *her* heart may the peace which passes understanding abide all the days of *her* life; through Jesus Christ our Lord. Amen.

For an Anniversary of Marriage

Loving God, we give thanks for the marriage of N. and N. for their time together and for the love they have shared with one another and with the world. We ask your blessing on their continuing years together and we pray that they may joyfully live out the promises made on their wedding day and that the love they share with one another may be a reflection of the love you share with us. Amen.

For a Civil Election

God of Justice, help us to discern wisely those we choose as leaders, and grant us grace to accept results we did not desire and the strength to never fail in advocating for a world of justice, peace, and mercy, Amen.

For a Congregational Election

God of Wisdom, as we prepare to choose the leaders of this community of faith, grant us discerning hearts and minds that we may choose wisely and that your will for us may be made complete. Amen.

For New, Continuing, and Departing Parish Leaders

Almighty God, you call us to serve your church as leaders and disciples. We thank you for the many wonderful ways our members serve this church, on the altar, in our offices and sacristy, behind the lectern, holding the chalice, amid the laughter of children, around tables, and in our community. Bless each person in their ministry, especially N. in thanksgiving for *their specific ministry* that they [*will begin, continue to do, are leaving now*] that they may feel the prayers and support of this parish, find joy in the calling to serve you in this, and know our gratitude. Amen.

For a Ministry of the Congregation

God of Mercy, we lift up before you the ministry of _____. Bless those who lead and those who labor on our behalf in this important work. Be present and lead them so that all they do may witness to your love. Amen.

For Those Serving in the Military

O Lord, watch over and protect those who serve on our behalf to defend and protect us. Grant them resilience and wisdom in the pursuit of their duties and return them to us safe and whole. Amen.

For Students Returning to School

Heavenly Father, we give you thanks for the ability to teach and to learn. On this day we especially pray for students and educators that are returning to school. Bless this school year with opportunities for growth, curiosity, creativity, and fun. Bless schools with safety and openness to new ideas. Bring your spirit of love into the classrooms, staff rooms, offices, libraries, gymnasiums, playgrounds, and dining halls of our community's schools and bless all those here with us today who will begin a new journey of learning this year. Amen.

INTRODUCTION

For a National Holiday

Loving God, to do your will is perfect freedom. As we celebrate our national founding, remind us that our highest allegiance belongs to Christ our Lord, and inspire us to work tirelessly to build a society and nation worthy of the promise of its founding; through Christ our redeemer, who with You and the Holy Spirit, lives and reigns, now and always. Amen.

For a Mass Shooting

Holy God, welcome the victims of the senseless murders in _place_ into your eternal embrace and mend the hearts and bodies broken by this horrific violence. Arouse our righteous anger and give us the wisdom and courage to find a path forward to a future without gun violence. Amen.

For a Community Health Crisis

Healing God, give us the strength and resilience to respond as a community to the threat of _issue_. Give wisdom to our public health authorities and all involved in defeating this crisis, and grant courage to our leaders to make decisions for the welfare and health of all people. Amen.

For Peace in a Time of War

Holy One, you cast a vision of a time when lions and lambs are brought together for safe slumber and where our instruments of war are remade into tools of peace. In this time of violence, war, and insecurity [_for ourselves, for our country, for name of country, for the world_], we beg that we might bring that vision to reality. Make us instruments of your peace and grant that we and all people may see an end to violence and a new reign of peace. Amen.

For a Natural Disaster

Merciful God, you know of the suffering in _place_ due to _disaster_. Give the people their strength to endure and give us generous hearts and willing hands that we might respond to their needs so that your benevolent grace might be known. Amen.

For Catechumens and Those Preparing for Baptism

O shepherd of our flock, we give thanks for those who hear your voice and answer your call, bless these persons, [N., N....] who seek to know you and to learn to walk your Way. Bless their learning and show us how to support them and discern with them the work you have called them to do in your Name. Amen.

Prayers for a New Priest or Deacon

Lord God, we thank you for bringing us to a new beginning with *N.N.*, our new *Rector/Priest/Deacon*. Bless our beginnings with *her* and open our hearts to allow room for change. We give thanks to you for our search team and our leadership for their work, and we commit ourselves to supporting this new relationship with *N.*, and *her* family. Lead us into new ways of being church, of serving the community and bind us together with strong bonds of love. Amen.

Principal Feasts & Holy Days

THE INCARNATION (CHRISTMAS)

All things have been clothed in grace by the incarnation of our Lord Jesus Christ; all the earth has been enlightened in his dawning. Trusting in His light and grace, let us pray for all people in need and for all the world, saying, Lord in your mercy, hear our prayer.

For the churches, which united they may be faithful in witness to your Son come among us.
Lord in your mercy, **hear our prayer.**

For the leaders of nations, that they may turn from ways of fear and warfare to the ways of your wisdom and grace.
Lord in your mercy, **hear our prayer.**

For the poor of the earth, for victims of violence and tyranny, that their suffering be ended, and that they may come to know joy.
Lord in your mercy, **hear our prayer.**

For all families, that they may be renewed in joy, receive the word of mercy into their hearts, and become places of hospitality to the stranger.
Lord in your mercy, **hear our prayer.**

For this congregation, that we may be renewed by the light and grace of your incarnate word.
Lord in your mercy, **hear our prayer.**

For those who have died, that their efforts continue to inspire our action and that they may rest in your care until that day when all shall rise again in your new Creation.
Lord in your mercy, **hear our prayer.**

Rejoicing in the company of Mary, mother of our Lord, and of all the witnesses of the incarnation, we commend these prayers and all our life to you, O God, through Jesus Christ our Lord. **Amen.**

THE HOLY NAME *January 1*

Lord God, hear us and respond to us, answer our needs that you may be glorified as we say, Lord in your mercy, hear our prayer.

Keep your church steadfast in its proclamation of the Good News of Jesus Christ in word and example and show us how to be your people with humility and grace.
Lord in your mercy, **hear our prayer.**

Inspire our action in the world, that we might influence our civil society to embody grace, charity, and generosity that we might lead the world into peace and the promotion of well-being for all people.
Lord in your mercy, **hear our prayer.**

Lead this assembly into wisdom and perseverance as we seek to follow in the example of Jesus and to go where He calls us.
Lord in your mercy, **hear our prayer.**

Open our hearts and minds that we might perceive new ways of being the faithful stewards of your creation that show our gratitude for the abundance you show us in nature.
Lord in your mercy, **hear our prayer.**

Give strength and resilience to those who suffer and bring wholeness and healing into their lives, especially we lift up those who have sought our prayers. [For...*prayer list.*]
Lord in your mercy, **hear our prayer.**

Hold fast to those who have died that they may bask in the glory of your eternal presence and grant us entry also into that place of light and life.
Lord in your mercy, **hear our prayer.**

Lord, we ask these prayers in the name of the one who was heralded by angels and whose name is the only one under heaven given for salvation, Jesus Christ, our Lord, and Savior who lives and reigns with you and the Holy Spirit, One God now and always. **Amen.**

THE EPIPHANY *January 6*

God of Love, arise, and shine in our hearts as we offer our prayers and praises to you saying, Lord in your mercy, hear our prayer.

Grant to the church wisdom to discern the presence of God in our midst and the courage to follow wherever it leads us.
Lord in your mercy, **hear our prayer.**

Bestow your blessing upon our nation, give our leaders loving hearts and concern for the least among us and embolden us to act out our faith in our common life.
Lord in your mercy, **hear our prayer.**

Be with us today and every day that your glory might show forth in our lives.
Lord in your mercy, **hear our prayer.**

We give thanks for the glories and abundance of creation, help us to cultivate gratitude in our hearts and souls that we might harvest generosity and love.
Lord in your mercy, **hear our prayer.**

Be present for all who suffer, give courage to the fearful, hope to the despairing, healing to the sick, wholeness to the injured, and comfort to the dying. [Especially we pray for...*prayer list.*]
Lord in your mercy, **hear our prayer.**

We pray that the dead might rest in your eternal care and that we too may enter into the glory of your presence in your new kingdom.
Lord in your mercy, **hear our prayer.**

Manifest God, may the example of Christ be our guide and His love the beacon of hope that ever draws us forward towards becoming the people you created us to be. **Amen.**

THE PRESENTATION *February 2*

Most Holy God, cast away the shadows in our lives that we might know the glory of your presence and hear and respond to our prayers that we might more fully live into your dreams for us as we say, Lord in your mercy, hear our prayer.

Guide your whole church into the light of your revelation and grant us the will and commitment to continue the mission of Jesus in our own lives.
Lord in your mercy, **hear our prayer.**

Grant the people of this nation the will and commitment to live in peace and to work in unity for the benefit of all people.
Lord in your mercy, **hear our prayer.**

Show us, gathered here today, the glory of your Son and help us discern more clearly your call on our lives that we might work in concert to work towards furthering the reign of Christ.
Lord in your mercy, **hear our prayer.**

Kindle in our hearts a sense of urgency and a firm commitment to be better stewards of your creation, that all future generations may know the abundance we have taken for granted.
Lord in your mercy, **hear our prayer.**

Be with all who suffer, relieve their distress, and bring healing to whatever needs mending in their bodies, souls, and mind. [Especially we pray for... *prayer list.*]

Lord in your mercy, **hear our prayer.**

Welcome the dying into your loving care and deal gently with all who grieve.
Lord in your mercy, **hear our prayer.**

In Christ we have seen your desire for our lives. Guide our feet and our hearts to truly live into His example that your hopes for humanity might be fulfilled. All these we ask through our Lord and intercessor, Jesus Christ who lives and reigns with you and the Holy Spirit, One God, now and always. **Amen.**

Apostles

ST MATTHIAS, *February 24*, Ss James and Philip *May 1*, St Barnabas, *June 11*, St James *July 25*, St Bartholomew *August 24*, Ss Simon and Jude *October 28*, St Andrew *November 30*, St Thomas, *December 21*

Hear us Lord as we say, Lord in your mercy, **hear our prayer.**

Your church is built upon the foundations established by the Apostles. May we ever bless their memory and seek to live into the example.
Lord in your mercy, **hear our prayer.**

Grant wisdom to the leaders of the nations that they might work together to further peace and the well-being of all people.
Lord in your mercy, **hear our prayer.**

Give us all an awareness of the part we can play in preserving the abundance of your creation and the courage to do it.
Lord in your mercy, **hear our prayer.**

Endow us gathered here with a growing love for Christ and a commitment to our faith that we might bring your glory to all whom we encounter and that we might fully know the joy of abundant life.
Lord in your mercy, **hear our prayer.**

Christ's name is the only name given under heaven for healing. Bring his healing presence to all who suffer that they may experience his peace.
Lord in your mercy, **hear our prayer.**

May all who have died enter into your eternal presence, and may we join them someday in your new age.
Lord in your mercy, **hear our prayer.**

Loving God, we give thanks for the example of your apostles, [especially N.]. May we also respond to the love of Christ and his command to bring the gospel to all people as they did, with courage and persistence. Through Christ our Lord and Advocate we pray. **Amen.**

SAINT JOSEPH *March 19*

Loving God, hear our prayers and answer us as we say, Lord in your mercy, hear our prayer.

Grant that all who lead your church may take up their vocations with the tender love and humility with which St Joseph took up his call to be the earthly father of Jesus.
Lord in your mercy, **hear our prayer.**

Enter into the hearts of all who hold authority in the world, that they might serve with integrity and devotion, seeking always the welfare of those in their charge.
Lord in your mercy, **hear our prayer.**

The whole world is your glorious creation, help us to preserve its abundant diversity that all future generations might know its bounty.
Lord in your mercy, **hear our prayer.**

Lead us gathered here to be your faithful servants, let us grow in faith and devotion to your Son, that all the world might know your glory through our actions.
Lord in your mercy, **hear our prayer.**

Let all who know illness, pain, brokenness, anxiety, or fear encounter Christ the healer who makes us whole and brings us peace.
Lord in your mercy, **hear our prayer.**

Bring into your glory all who have died that they may rest in your eternal embrace and bring us also into your loving presence when our time to depart comes.
Lord in your mercy, **hear our prayer.**

Your servant Joseph trusted in you despite his doubts and fears and came to love your Son as his own. Give us faith like Joseph's that we may overcome our fears and doubts through our trust in you and come to know and love your Son, our Lord, with our whole selves. **Amen.**

THE ANNUNCIATION *March 25*

We lift our hearts and voices to you in devotion and faith, calling out your glory as we say, Lord in your mercy, hear our prayer.

Remind your church that greatness in the world is not a sign of greatness in your eyes. Keep us humble and faithfully devoted to sharing the Good News of Jesus.
Lord in your mercy, **hear our prayer.**

Be in the hearts of the leaders of the world, guide them into peace, and open them to perceive that the way of unity and cooperation is the surest path to human thriving for all.
Lord in your mercy, **hear our prayer.**

The challenges of the world can only be addressed through the accumulation of our individual small choices. Bestow upon wisdom and courage to make those choices rightly that all future generations may know the full glory of your creation.
Lord in your mercy, **hear our prayer.**

May the courage and commitment of Mary be shared by all in this assembly, that our faithful actions might also make Christ manifest in the world.
Lord in your mercy, **hear our prayer.**

Grant relief and peace to all who know any suffering or distress, that your light of love may dispel the darkness of pain and suffering.
Lord in your mercy, **hear our prayer.**

Help us to remember that death is the gateway to eternal life. Comfort us who grieve, give courage to us who are near the end, and welcome us all into the glory of your presence in our time.
Lord in your mercy, **hear our prayer.**

Lord in the answer of Mary to your calling to be the Christ-bearer, you have given us a wonderful example of a courageous faithfulness without fear. Grant that we too may hear and answer your calls upon our lives that your kingdom might be made manifest in our lives. **Amen.**

Evangelists

ST MARK *April 25*, ST MATTHEW *September 21*, ST LUKE *October 18*, ST JOHN *December 28*

We lift up a chorus of praise and faithfulness in prayer as we say, Lord in your mercy, hear our prayer.

Grant to all who preach and teach in your church integrity to your Word and a faithful desire to bring all people to the feast of the Lamb.
Lord in your mercy, **hear our prayer.**

Establish peace in this world, quell the hatred that lurks in human hearts, and let us be the bearers of love and light to our neighbors.
Lord in your mercy, **hear our prayer.**

Teach us to tread softly as we walk through your creation, learning to preserve its glory, beauty, and abundance for all future generations.
Lord in your mercy, **hear our prayer.**

Give us a love for your Word and a devotion to its teachings that our lives might be lived more fully in the example of Jesus.
Lord in your mercy, **hear our prayer.**

Bring peace and wholeness to all who suffer or are broken. Mend what is amiss in our lives.
Lord in your mercy, **hear our prayer.**

Refine the souls of all who have died that they may grow into the goodness of their creation and be with you eternally offering praise and resting in joyful peace.
Lord in your mercy, **hear our prayer.**

Through the Evangelists, you have given us the ability to encounter and know our Ord and redeemer, Jesus. We give thanks for their sharing of the word, [especially N.]. May we read, mark, learn, and inwardly digest their gospels that we may learn to recognize Christ's presence with us. **Amen.**

THE ASCENSION

Holy Christ, we praise you and give thanks for your presence with the father and your intercessions on our behalf, offering our prayers in humility and hope as we say, Lord in your mercy, hear our prayer.

You have built and empowered your church to continue your ministry, commanding us to carry your example into the future, grant us discerning hearts that we might fulfill your commandments in faith and humility.
Lord in your mercy, **hear our prayer.**

Be with the leaders of the nations, bend their hearts that they may work together to pursue peace and human thriving.
Lord in your mercy, **hear our prayer.**

Form in us hearts of love that we might serve our neighbors with generosity and without fear.
Lord in your mercy, **hear our prayer.**

We offer thanks for the abundant glory of creation, incline our hearts to respect the natural world and give us wisdom to use its resources sustainably.
Lord in your mercy, **hear our prayer.**

Let your healing presence be felt by all who suffer. Bring healing to the sick, courage to the oppressed, and hope to the dispirited.
Lord in your mercy, **hear our prayer.**

You have invited all to the feast of the new kingdom, grant that we all may thankfully respond with a resounding Yes! that we and all whom we love but see no more may arise in your heavenly kingdom,
Lord in your mercy, **hear our prayer.**

Holy God, you have empowered us to be Christ's body in the world, through us may the world know the loving embrace of Him, who with you and the Holy Spirit live and reigns, now and always. **Amen.**

THE VISITATION *May 31*

We offer up our needs and the hopes of our hearts as together we say, Lord in your mercy, hear our prayer.

May your church always embody the joy of the presence of Christ that we may with spirits uplifted undertake the work of the Gospel.
Lord in your mercy, **hear our prayer.**

Lead the people of this nation to the ways of justice and mercy, that we might know not merely the absence of strife and conflict but the deep and true peacefulness of mutual respect and love.
Lord in your mercy, **hear our prayer.**

We glory in the bounty of creation and bless all who work to sustain its abundance for us and for all future generations.
Lord in your mercy, **hear our prayer.**

May the Spirit of God touch the hearts of all gathered here and inspire us to more closely and faithfully follow wherever Christ leads us.
Lord in your mercy, **hear our prayer.**

Mend what is broken, heal what is sick, bring to wholeness what has been diminished. Bring your healing power into our lives and into the lives of all who suffer.
Lord in your mercy, **hear our prayer.**

Grant an entrance into your loving care to all who have died, that your promises of old might be fulfilled for all people.
Lord in your mercy, **hear our prayer.**

Mary and Elizabeth gave birth to your embodied promises. So grant us faith and commitment to continue the ministry of Jesus that we too may give birth to your loving promises to those in our lives. **Amen.**

NATIVITY OF ST JOHN THE BAPTIST *June 24*

Hear the prayers of your people and respond to us as may be best for us and for the furtherance of your glory as we say, Lord in your mercy, hear our prayer.

May your church ever be a herald for the coming of the Good News that its every action might further the reign of God in human lives.
Lord in your mercy, **hear our prayer.**

May our nation be a place where opportunities are available to all people to live into the potential with which you lovingly created them.
Lord in your mercy, **hear our prayer.**

Unite the people of the world that together we might courageously face and overcome our global challenges.
Lord in your mercy, **hear our prayer.**

Grant that this assembly might grow strong in the Spirit and be bearers of light to those who sit in the shadows of fear and despair.
Lord in your mercy, **hear our prayer.**

Lift up those who are weighed down by sickness, injury, oppression, fear, and despair. Grant them wholeness and the healing power of your presence.
Lord in your mercy, **hear our prayer.**

May all who have died be swiftly brought into your eternal presence and may those who grieve find comfort in the knowledge of your eternal embrace.
Lord in your mercy, **hear our prayer.**

In Christ you have raised up a might savior and fulfilled your ancient promises. Grant that we may be faithful in proclaiming the life- and world-changing power of his presence among us. **Amen.**

SS PETER AND PAUL *June 29*

Hear us Lord and answer as we say, Lord in your mercy, hear our prayer.

Grant your church the courage and persistence of Peter and Paul, that we, like them, might carry the love of Christ everywhere we go.
Lord, in your mercy, **hear our prayer.**

Embolden us to work with our fellow citizens to build a society rooted in justice, mercy, and care for the least among us, that all might have an opportunity to thrive.
Lord, in your mercy, **hear our prayer.**

Help us to see that care for creation is caring for your people, that we are inseparable from the creation in which we were made to live.
Lord, in your mercy, **hear our prayer.**

Bless this assembly with deeper faith that we might be without fear and willing to be bold for the sake of the gospel.
Lord in your mercy, **hear our prayer.**

Grant relief of pain, sickness, and anxiety to all who suffer. Bring your healing power to bear and mend what is broken in our lives.
Lord in your mercy, **hear our prayer.**

Welcome those who have died into the assembly of saints which surround you in glory and grant a hopeful peace to those who grieve.
Lord in your mercy, **hear our prayer.**

In Peter and Paul, you lifted up leaders who loved fiercely and worked tirelessly for your sake. May their example be an inspiration to us who seek to make Christ the model of our lives. **Amen.**

ST MARY MAGDALENE *July 22*

Help us to you are present among us as we raise our voice in prayer saying, Lord in your mercy, hear our prayer.

Open the eyes of your church to recognize that the voices of the marginalized are your voices and that you often enter into our lives from unexpected places.
Lord in your mercy, **hear our prayer.**

Bring peace to our world, let us be instruments of reconciliation in all areas and places of conflict, that we may no longer call one another enemy.
Lord in your mercy, **hear our prayer.**

Show us the way to reimagine our relationship to creation that we might value preservation above exploitation and see ourselves as caretakers instead of consumers.
Lord in your mercy, **hear our prayer.**

Grace this assembly with your presence in our lives and lead us into the glorious embrace of your love.
Lord in your mercy, **hear our prayer.**

Lord, as you healed Mary of Magdala, bring healing to all who suffer in this world, grant them peace and relief from their pain.
Lord in your mercy, **hear our prayer.**

Bring all who have died into perfection in the glory of your presence, grant peace to all who grieve, and allow us also to join, at the end of our earthly journey, with the saints who surround you eternally.
Lord in your mercy, **hear our prayer.**

Loving God, you called Mary Magdalene to be witness to the Apostles showing us that you love knows no partiality. Help us also to love others as Christ loves us. All this we offer in the name of our Lord and Savior, Jesus Christ who lives and reigns with you and the Holy Spirit, One God, now and forever. **Amen.**

US INDEPendence Day *July 4*

Let us lift our voices in praise and prayer by saying, Lord in your mercy, hear our prayer.

Let you church be a true expression of the love and example of Christ that it may grow in influence and be a model for all people who seek to live in peace and serve those in need.
Lord in your mercy, **hear our prayer.**

Aid our nation in learning to live more fully into its promise. Bring her promises to all who live here that every person may be treated with dignity and where all our children may grow into their potential.
Lord in your mercy, **hear our prayer.**

Grant wisdom and determination to our leaders that this nation might be a leader in developing sustainable ways of being and answering the challenges of climate change.
Lord in your mercy, **hear our prayer.**

Help us to remember that we are citizens of the kingdom of God foremost and embolden us to enter into civic life to be advocates for Christ's way of peace, justice, and mercy.
Lord in your mercy, **hear our prayer.**

Bring relief to our neighbors who are denied opportunities and who are prevented from accessing the promises of our national life and bring healing and peace to all who suffer from illness and injury.
Lord in your mercy, **hear our prayer.**

May those who died rest in peace and rise again in your new age to live the promised life of Christ.
Lord in your mercy, **hear our prayer.**

We give thanks for the liberties and freedoms promised to us and celebrated on this Independence Day. Help us to use these gifts wisely and for the benefit of all people as shown us by the example of our Lord and Savior Jesus Christ, in whose name these prayers are offered. **Amen.**

ST MARY THE VIRGIN *August 15*

With trust in your mercy O God, we lift our voices to you as we pray, Lord in your mercy, hear our prayer.

May the quiet confidence and loving devotion of Mary, the mother of our Lord, always be present in your church.
Lord in your mercy, **hear our prayer.**

May our nation be led by those humbly dedicated to lifting up the lowly and establishing peace and justice for all.
Lord in your mercy, **hear our prayer.**

May the hearts of all people be moved to embrace ways of being that surmount our challenges and bring about a prosperous and sustainable way of life.
Lord in your mercy, **hear our prayer.**

May we who are gathered here have trust enough in you to overcome our fears as blessed Mary did and follow where you ask us to go for the furtherance of your salvation.
Lord in your mercy, **hear our prayer.**

May all who are sick or injured, or in need of peace and freedom-from-worry, encounter and be transformed by the healing love of Christ.
Lord in your mercy, **hear our prayer.**

May all who have died be met with your tender love and rise again in the new age, and may we share with them in your eternal glory.
Lord in your mercy, **hear our prayer.**

In the devotion of Mary, the Christ-Bearer, you have stablished for all time a standard of love and faith that inspires us and gives a model that we can follow. Hear and answer our prayers as may be best for us but always to your glory. All that we ask, we ask through Christ our redeemer and Lord. **Amen.**

THE TRANSFIGURATION *August 6*

Formed by the word and promise of God, let us pray that the merciful glory of God, manifest in all the earth, may drive away all darkness as we say, Lord, in your mercy, hear our prayer

For the church of Christ, that knowing now only in part, we may wait in humility and joy to see your full light. and that God's providence may lead all people from death into life.
Lord in your mercy, hear our prayer.

For and all who minister in your name, that they may speak clearly of your Christ in their words and actions, so that our lives may be transformed,
Lord in your mercy, hear our prayer.

For those just beginning to walk the path of Christ, and those who have long tread that path, that we may always remember that faith is a journey,
Lord in your mercy, hear our prayer.

For the nations of the earth and for their leaders, that they may know and practice the ways of peace,
Lord in your mercy, hear our prayer.

For all those who seek you, knowingly or not, that they will find the everlasting mercy and never-ending love of the One who has called them by name,
Lord in your mercy, hear our prayer.

For the sick and suffering, and all who have asked our prayers, that they may find healing and wholeness,
Lord in your mercy, hear our prayer.

For those who have died, that may endure in your loving care until they rise again in the new age of Christ,
Lord in your mercy, hear our prayer.

You are present on mountaintops and in valleys, be with us always and deliver us into the peace of your promise, abundant and eternal life, that we may be emboldened to love and serve without fear. **Amen.**

HOLY CROSS DAY *September 14*

Holy God, our souls stand bare in contemplation of the atoning sacrifice completed upon the cross of Christ, may our hearts tremble at His love as we lift our voices in prayer and say, Lord in your mercy, hear our prayer.

May your church, like Christ, forever open its arms in embrace that all may know His love and follow his example.
Lord in your mercy, **hear our prayer.**

Fill the hearts of the leaders of the world that they might be willing to lay aside their desires in order to bring peace and well-being to all the people of every nation.
Lord in your mercy, **hear our prayer.**

Give us all a sense of devotion and duty to your call for us to be stewards of earthly abundance, that we might create a prosperous and sustainable future.
Lord in your mercy, **hear our prayer.**

Inspire this assembly to take up their crosses and follow where Jesus leads so that the light of his victory might swallow up the shadows of evil in our own lives and in our own community.
Lord in your mercy, **hear our prayer.**

Be with those who suffer in any way, that they might feel your healing presence and no release from their trials.
Lord in your mercy, **hear our prayer.**

Embrace those who have died in your loving arms that they may know eternal peace and love.
Lord in your mercy, **hear our prayer.**

Through the faith of Christ on the cross, He has opened to us the path of eternal life, may his light and beckoning call draw us fearlessly into service for the sake of the gospel. Through that same Christ, our Lord, we pray. **Amen.**

Martyrs

ST JAMES OF JERUSALEM *October 23*, St Stephen, *December 26*

Almighty God, we join our voices with all you surround your throne as we say, Lord in your mercy, hear our prayer.

Grant to your church the eternal memory of your martyrs, and may it always be led by those willing to give it their full devotion and love.
Lord in your mercy, **hear our prayer.**

Grant us energy and wisdom to be engaged citizens and advocates for the gospel imperatives of peace and the recognition of the dignity of all persons.
Lord in your mercy, **hear our prayer.**

Grant us persistence and courage to pursue a reimagined way of life that brings us and all future generations sustainable prosperity.
Lord in your mercy, **hear our prayer.**

Grant to this assembly the desire to love and serve you by loving and serving one another and carrying together that love and service to our neighbors.
Lord in your mercy, **hear our prayer.**

Grant peace and wholeness to all who suffer in body, mind, or spirit through the healing power of Christ's presence.
Lord in your mercy, **hear our prayer.**

Grant to the dying a peaceful end and a place among your faithful in your eternal and glorious presence.
Lord in your mercy, **hear our prayer.**

We are thankful for the devotion and witness of the martyrs [especially N.]. May we also give ourselves wholly to the gospel imperative to love you and our neighbors with all that we are, and we offer these prayers in the name of our Lord and Savior, Jesus Christ. **Amen.**

ST MICHAEL AND ALL ANGELS *September 19*

With the angels and archangels who surround your throne we lift our voices in praise and prayer as we say, Lord in your mercy, hear our prayer.

Send your angels to protect your Church from error and to help us stay true to Christ's command to love and serve.
Lord in your mercy, **hear our prayer.**

Inspire our national imagination to seek the best in one another and to work together to build a more perfect union.
Lord in your mercy, **hear our prayer.**

As the angels are devoted to You, may we also be devoted to care of your creation and for building a sustainable world for all future generations.
Lord in your mercy, **hear our prayer.**

Open our ears to hear the holy messengers that enter into our lives and may we work together to make this community a place of refuge and a safe harbor from which to launch God's loving Word into the world.
Lord in your mercy, **hear our prayer.**

Open our hearts to the suffering in the world and in our own lives, let us be servants and encouragers to all in need of Christ's healing power.
Lord in your mercy, **hear our prayer.**

Embrace all who have died and grant them an entrance that they may sing with all your angels of the glory of God and bask in the love of your eternal presence.
Lord in your mercy, **hear our prayer.**

Holy God, you have graced our lives with messengers of your love, let us always be mindful of the angels in our presence and heed their words that your glory may be reflected through our lives. **Amen.**

ALL SAINTS *November 1*

Immersed in the loving cloud of witnesses we offer our prayers with joy and hope as we say, Lord in your mercy, hear our prayer.

May your church pursue its ministry and proclaim the good news with integrity, humility, and courage, that the whole world may come to know the love of Christ.
Lord in your mercy, **hear our prayer.**

May our nation be a place of peace and opportunity where all people might thrive and be free to pursue their potential, and be blessed with leaders who pursue the common good and work for the health of the whole nation.
Lord in your mercy, **hear our prayer.**

Kindle hope and courage in the hearts of this assembly that we might continue the good work of those who came before and someday pass on our mission to generations to come, that we might be an unbroken link in the chain of faith.
Lord in your mercy, **hear our prayer.**

Give us courage to face our global challenges with open hearts, open minds, and a willingness to take on new and sustainable ways of living in your creation.
Lord in your mercy, **hear our prayer.**

Mend what is broken, heal what is amiss, and bring wholeness and peace to all people that we might live the abundant life of Christ.
Lord in your mercy, **hear our prayer.**

We are surrounded by the love of those who have entered already into your eternal care, grant us to one day join them in that great cloud of witnesses and to be an inspiration today to those who will be your church on earth tomorrow.
Lord in your mercy, **hear our prayer.**

God, you have cared for us since we first drew breath and walked the earth, continue to be with us and to lead us into an ever-greater awareness of you that our lives may be reflect your loving glory into the world. **Amen.**

THANKSGIVING DAY *Fourth Thursday in November*

With grateful hearts we offer our deepest needs and desires to you as we say, Lord in your mercy, hear our prayer.

Give to your church a perpetual awareness of the blessing of this life and gift of Christ's sacrificial love that we may take up our ministries with thankfulness and joy.
Lord in your mercy, **hear our prayer.**

Make us mindful of the possibilities of this day, that we may forever recognize strength in diversity and the potential of cooperation where there is mistrust and fear.
Lord in your mercy, **hear our prayer.**

As we celebrate the bounty of creation and embrace the gifts of relationship, keep us ever mindful of those who are without and show us how work together to ensure that the circle of your love expands ever outward.
Lord in your mercy, **hear our prayer.**

Bless this assembly with humble and grateful hearts and empower them to be the bringers of the light of Christ's love into the shadows of sin and evil.
Lord in your mercy, **hear our prayer.**

Remember all who are sick and suffering in any way, bring them healing and peace and show us how we might be servants in your healing work.
Lord in your mercy, **hear our prayer.**

Welcome the dying, comfort those in grief, and let us all anticipate the end of our earthly lives with quiet confidence in the promises of our Lord, Jesus Christ.
Lord in your mercy, **hear our prayer.**

Giving thanks for the blessings of this life and mindful of the work still needed to ensure the dignity and well-being of all people, we praise you Lord for the gift of Christ's atoning sacrifice and the opportunity to know, love and serve you. These prayers we offer in the name of the same Lord, Jesus, who lives and reigns with you and the Holy Spirit now and always. **Amen.**

Lectionary Year A

FIRST SUNDAY OF ADVENT

Let us now open our hearts and offer to God our deepest prayers as we say, Lord in your mercy, hear our prayers.

Heavenly Father, inspire the universal church to be most concerned with living lives inspired by your Son and give us hearts that beat to serve you.
Lord in your mercy, **hear our prayer.**

Bless those in authority, in this nation and in all the nations, with an urgency to care for all people and to undo systems of injustice.
Lord in your mercy, **hear our prayer.**

Give us opportunities to live into our faith and identity as followers of Jesus. Open our eyes to see those around us, in our neighborhoods, schools, and places of work, who need our loving support and care.
Lord in your mercy, **hear our prayer.**

Grant wisdom and persistence to those who seek cures and relief of pain, and heal and comfort those who suffer from illness. [Especially for… *prayer list.*]
Lord in your mercy, **hear our prayer.**

Give us wisdom and persistence for the care of creation.
Lord in your mercy, **hear our prayer.**

Grant rest eternal to those who have died and comfort to those who mourn. Grant us daily an awareness that life is precious and fleeting, that we might use our hours to your glory.
Lord in your mercy, **hear our prayer.**

Almighty God, you lovingly created and care for us, hear now these prayers and answer them as may be best for us and for the furtherance of your redemptive grace. **Amen.**

SECOND SUNDAY OF ADVENT

Holy God, yours is the voice that calls from the places we least expect, inviting us into ever deeper relationship with you that we might live surrounded by your love. Hear now our prayers as we say, Lord in your mercy, hear our prayers.

We pray for Christ's church, that we may never become settled in comfort but that we might always be on pilgrimage serving those we encounter.
Lord in your mercy, **hear our prayer.**

We pray for those who hold authority over us, that they might escape from their fears and hatreds and govern in the glory of your mercy and wisdom.
Lord in your mercy, **hear our prayer.**

We pray for each other in this parish community, that we might discern our own calls to be Christ in all the places our day-to-day lives take us.
Lord in your mercy, **hear our prayer.**

We pray for the natural world and for our own stewardship of creation, that we might be advocates for actions needed to leave an abundant creation to future generations.
Lord in your mercy, **hear our prayer.**

We pray for all in need of healing and relief from their burdens, worries, and fears. [Especially we lift up…*prayer list.*]
Lord in your mercy, **hear our prayer.**

We pray for those who have died and those who grieve, hasten the day of Christ's return that we might be reunited with all whom we have loved but see no more.
Lord in your mercy, **hear our prayer.**

Almighty God, you entered into our world and blessed our lives through the life, death, and resurrection of Christ, your son and our Lord. Bless us still as we strive to become the people we were meant to be. **Amen.**

THIRD SUNDAY OF ADVENT

O Lord who has created and loved us and who calls to us be still and wait. Heed our prayers as we say, Lord in your mercy, hear our prayer

Help us to hear and to accept gratefully your call to be God's people, ignoring the glory and favor of this world in favor of the glory of the kingdom of God.
Lord in your mercy, **hear our prayer.**

Turn us away from our fears and division and teach us to embrace your promise, that ours might be a nation of hope and generosity. Lord in your mercy, **hear our prayer.**

Open our eyes to the majesty of your creation and strengthen our resolve to preserve its abundance for the sustenance of all future generations.
Lord in your mercy, **hear our prayer.**

Lead us to where your loving presence is most needed and help us to be your agents of love to our neighbors.
Lord in your mercy, **hear our prayer.**

Enter into the lives of all who suffer, that they might draw strength from your presence. [Especially we ask for your healing powers in the lives of… *prayer list.*]
Lord in your mercy, **hear our prayer.**

Deal tenderly with those who are grieving and with those whose wounds from loss are reopened at this time of year. May we feel the assurance of your promises that we will be reunited in your glorious presence in the new age.
Lord in your mercy, **hear our prayer.**

Almighty God, in the face of Christ we see the fullness of your love for us, help us to be the people you created us to be and to live fully in the light of your countenance. All this we ask in the name of Lord, Jesus Christ who with You and the Holy Spirit, lives and reigns, One God, now and always. **Amen.**

FOURTH SUNDAY OF ADVENT

Loving God, you know our needs more deeply than we can ever know them ourselves. Open our eyes to see as you do, that we may know your peace and grace in our own lives. Bend our hearts through our prayer to know you and to love you more perfectly, as we say, Lord in your mercy, hear our prayer.

Help those who follow you to see in each other the fullness of Christ, that we might work together in joy to further your vision for our world.
Lord in your mercy, **hear our prayer.**

Protect and bless your church in all its diversity and grant wisdom and strength to those who guide and shape its life.
Lord in your mercy, **hear our prayer**

Shower your blessings on the leaders of the nations, that they might seek solutions to the world's problems through peaceful cooperation.
Lord in your mercy, **hear our prayer.**

Help us to be witnesses to your promises in our own communities, that your glory might be reflected through us, that all may know the possibilities of your loving way, and guard and protect all who will be travelling in this time of celebration, be present to those who feel alone or forgotten, and comfort those who are reminded of their griefs.
Lord in your mercy, **hear our prayer.**

Bring wholeness to what is broken, relief to what causes pain, and healing to our illnesses. Lift up all who suffer that they may find peace through you. [Especially we remember...*prayer list.*]
Lord in your mercy, **hear our prayer.**

Assure us of your loving care for those who have died and bolster our faith that we may be reunited with them again someday.
Lord in your mercy, **hear our prayer.**

You have loved us enough to take on human life as your own and to know our hopes and our fears. Hear now our prayers and fulfill them as may be best for us and all of this we ask through your Son, our Lord and advocate, Jesus Christ. **Amen.**

LECTIONARY YEAR A

FIRST SUNDAY AFTER CHRISTMAS

Heavenly Father, we are your children, formed and created for love. Give us hearts that see our neighbors as our true brothers and sisters, that we might care for one another as you care for us and hear our prayers as we say Lord in your mercy, hear our prayer.

We pray for all those who worship you in the church universal, that the good news might be proclaimed, lives enriched, and hands put into service for those in need, all that your name might be known and glorified.
Lord, in your mercy, **hear our prayer.**

We pray for our nation and its leaders, and for all nations, that you will be the guiding force that directs all decisions and actions for the benefit of all the world.
Lord, in your mercy, **hear our prayer.**

We pray for our planet, that your peace might prevail, that your love might win over all hearts. We pray that the abundance of this life might be shared with those who have little and that the plight of the persecuted might become untenable for those who live in plenty.
Lord, in your mercy, **hear our prayer.**

We pray for our own personal needs and concerns, for those we love, for those we mourn, for the success of our labor and the needs of our own families, asking you to be present to us and to those we love this day and every day.
Lord, in your mercy, **hear our prayer.**

We pray for those who are afraid, who hunger, who are imprisoned in cells or by illness or addiction. We pray for certainty, shelter, food, liberation, and healing and for the peace of those whose needs are known to you alone.
Lord, in your mercy, **hear our prayer.**

We pray for the sick and the dying. [Especially we pray for...*prayer list.*] We pray also for those who mourn and those who offer comfort, for the release of fear and the increase of faith, and for our hope of life eternal lived in your presence.
Lord, in your mercy, **hear our prayer.**

Abba, Father, hear our prayers offered in the security of your love and grant them not as we desire but as may be best for us. **Amen.**

SECOND SUNDAY After Christmas

Creator God, you have formed us for purpose. Enter more deeply into our hearts that we might more fully know you and the role you have created us for, and accept our prayers as we say, Lord in your mercy, hear our prayer.

Empower your church to speak truth and to stand boldly against the dark powers of this world, that it might be a refuge and a place for hope.
Lord in your mercy, **hear our prayer.**

Embolden your people to hold to account the leaders of the world, that they might pursue policies of peace and international fellowship.
Lord in your mercy, **hear our prayer.**

Grant us discerning and generous hearts that your blessings might be made known to our neighbors through our actions.
Lord in your mercy, **hear our prayer.**

Equip us and sustain us to forestall environmental catastrophe, and to preserve the glorious abundance of creation for future generations.
Lord in your mercy, **hear our prayer.**

Support those who suffer and make your healing presence known to them.
[Especially we pray for…*prayer list.*]
Lord in your mercy, **hear our prayer.**

Accept the dying into your loving arms and greet us also in the hour of our deaths that we might rise again in your new age.
Lord in your mercy, **hear our prayer.**

Speak to us and guide us in our life's path so that we might be fully the people you created us to be. All we have and all we ask comes from you, O Lord who with the Son and Holy Spirit, reigns forever, One God. **Amen.**

FIRST SUNDAY AFTER EPIPHANY

Heavenly Father, in gratitude for the message of love you sent to us in the word made flesh, Jesus, your Son, we offer you the longings of our hearts as we say, Lord in your mercy, hear our prayer.

We pray for your church, for all who find you there, for those who love you and for those who long to love you more. Give us a spirit of invitation, and the courage to find new ways to be good news to all your people.
Lord in your mercy, **hear our prayer.**

We pray for the nation and for all who govern. We pray for our future and the future of all nations and peoples, that we may be united in the desire for peace and life for everyone.
Lord in your mercy, **hear our prayer.**

We pray for the world and its needs, for the state of our oceans and soil; the survival of your creatures and the safety of all people and that those who are able will work diligently for liberation and sustenance.
Lord in your mercy, **hear our prayer.**

We pray for the needs of the communities we call home and our neighbors, for those we know and those who are strangers to us. We give you thanks for our adoption, which makes us brothers and sisters in Christ.
Lord in your mercy, **hear our prayer.**

We pray for those who are ill or injured, and for those who are depressed and anxious, that they may know the comfort of your healing love and the joy of each new day. [Especially we ask healing for...*prayer list*.]
Lord in your mercy, **hear our prayer.**

We pray for the dying, for those who labor to leave this world, that their departing may be peaceful and fearless. We pray also for those who weep this day and those who mourn the dead.
Lord in your mercy, **hear our prayer.**

Offering you these prayers and praises we acknowledge our dependence on you alone. Uphold us this day and every day and to bless our endeavors as we strive to bring about your kingdom vision for this world. We ask all this in the name of your Son, who lives and reigns with you, and the Holy Spirit, one God now and forever. **Amen.**

SECOND SUNDAY AFTER EPIPHANY

God of strength and resoluteness, you have sought to make yourself known to us and to show us your loving care. Hear our collective hopes and prayers as we say, Lord in your mercy, hear our prayer.

Encourage the truth speakers and prophets of your church, that we might see the Christ in our midst.
Lord in your mercy, **hear our prayer.**

Be with the leaders of our nation. Hold them accountable to their commitments to liberty, peace, and unity.
Lord in your mercy, **hear our prayer.**

Grant us the wisdom, strength, and perseverance to make difficult decisions for the welfare of creation.
Lord in your mercy, **hear our prayer.**

Heal those in pain or illness. Bring joy to the sorrowful, hope to the forlorn. Grant a path to your promise to all who have lost their way. [Especially we pray for...*prayer list.*]
Lord in your mercy, **hear our prayer.**

Guide us as we seek to become icons of Christ and builders of the kingdom of God in all the places our lives take us.
Lord in your mercy, **hear our prayer.**

Bring peace to the dying and comfort to those who grieve. Grant us all a new life in your eternal presence
Lord in your mercy, **hear our prayer.**

You Son lived and died as one of us that we might know the surest path to the life we were created for. Let the light of his love shine in our lives, dispelling all darkness and leading us ever forward into your glory. **Amen.**

THIRD SUNDAY AFTER EPIPHANY

We pray to you Holy God, in the confidence of our belovedness as we say, Lord in your mercy, hear our prayer.

We give thanks for the multitude of the faithful who have offered you their lives in faith. Bless the universal church with a resounding chorus of affirmation and fill us with shared affection and true purpose to bring your kingdom nearer still.
Lord in your mercy, **hear our prayer.**

We pray to you for our nation and for our elected leaders in city, state, and national government, that our country and all countries might look to you and your way of love.
Lord in your mercy, **hear our prayer.**

We pray for the welfare of all people, for those we see as allies and for those we fear, that all might know peace in their heart.
Lord in your mercy, **hear our prayer.**

We pray for the concerns and worries of our hearts. Be present to us and lead us into faith, contentment, and joy.
Lord in your mercy, **hear our prayer.**

We pray for those who suffer in body, mind, or spirit that they will seek and find you in their distress. [Especially we pray for…*prayer list.*]
Lord in your mercy, **hear our prayer.**

We pray for the departed, for those who are dying and those who watch and weep. Bring peace and comfort to the grieving and the hope of life eternal to those who labor on toward your kingdom.
Lord in your mercy, **hear our prayer.**

Be our strong shield and certain companion in this and every day, that we might know and love you more: Father Son and Holy Spirit. **Amen.**

FOURTH SUNDAY AFTER EPIPHANY

God of blessings hear our prayers and act swiftly to answer them as we say, Lord in your mercy, hear our prayer.

Embolden your church, that it may fearlessly accept its mission to bring light and love into the world without judgement.
Lord in your mercy, **hear our prayer.**

Keep the needs of the most vulnerable foremost in the minds and in the intentions of our elected leaders and public servants, that the dignity of all may be preserved and the welfare of our whole nation increased.
Lord in your mercy, **hear our prayer.**

Help us to ground our choices in our concern for those most impacted by climate change and in the need to preserve the abundance of creation for future generations.
Lord in your mercy, **hear our prayer.**

Shower your blessing on this congregation that they might know and feel your presence in their lives and act in the confidence of your love for the good of all.
Lord in your mercy, **hear our prayer.**

Bring wholeness and peace to all who suffer, free them from their afflictions and instill in them the hope of Christ. [Especially we pray for... *prayer list.*]
Lord in your mercy, **hear our prayer.**

Welcome in your embrace all those who have died and so guide our lives that we may confidently look forward to our reunion with them and you.
Lord in your mercy, **hear our prayer.**

God of true wisdom who through Christ has given us the model of human life, so inspire us that we might live always in the joy of our salvation and greet with joy the day of your coming. **Amen.**

FIFTH SUNDAY AFTER EPIPHANY

Creating God, you have made us in your image that we might reflect your glory, hear us now as we say, Lord in your mercy, hear our prayer.

Be present in and guide your church that it might always stand for the way that leads to life and light.
Lord in your mercy, **hear our prayer.**

Grant your wisdom and mercy to all who hold authority in our lives that their leadership might benefit all people and bring about a just and equitable world.
Lord in your mercy, **hear our prayer.**

We offer to you the deepest needs and longings of our own hearts, help us to grow into the people you created us to be and to take up the work you have given us to do.
Lord in your mercy, **hear our prayer.**

Open our eyes to behold the glory of your Creation that we might take up our responsibilities to preserve and protect it with joy.
Lord in your mercy, **hear our prayer.**

Extend your healing presence to all who suffer and restore them to a sense of wholeness. [Especially we pray for...*prayer list.*]
Lord in your mercy, **hear our prayer.**

Welcome all who have died into your loving presence and bring us also into that new kingdom in your new age.
Lord in your mercy, **hear our prayer.**

You have offered us the gift of grace and reconciliation through the life, death, and resurrection of Christ. Let us live into your Son's example that we might also know abundant life in your presence. All we ask, we ask through our Lord and intercessor, who with you and Holy Spirit lives reigns eternally. **Amen.**

SIXTH SUNDAY AFTER EPIPHANY

Holy God, we hold fast to your promise to be with us. Hear now our prayers as we say, Lord in your mercy, hear our prayer.

We manifest your promises through the faithful work of your universal church. Strengthen and guide us to be the bearers of your good news.

Lord in your mercy, **hear our prayer.**

Be with our nation and its elected leaders. Blanket them and us in your wisdom and compassion. Help us to build a world that offers security, peace, prosperity, and a home for everyone.
Lord in your mercy, **hear our prayer.**

Guide us gathered here today into being the agents of your love in all the places of our daily lives.
Lord in your mercy, **hear our prayer.**

Preserve this world in peace and protect the earth and its creatures from our sin. Keep us mindful that we are called to be stewards of your creation. Grant us the ability to change course and begin to repair the damage our greed and apathy have allowed.
Lord in your mercy, **hear our prayer.**

Be present to those ailing in body, mind, or spirit, and especially to those who pray even now for hope, for cure, or for peace. [Especially we pray for…*prayer list.*]
Lord in your mercy, **hear our prayer.**

Grant to the departed release from the worries and cares of this world and bring them with all your saints into the glory of your eternal care.
Lord in your mercy, **hear our prayer.**

We offer these prayers with all those who call on you to lend salt and light to this life, in the name of your son, Jesus, who with you and the Holy Spirit lives and reigns, one God, forever and ever. **Amen.**

SEVENTH SUNDAY AFTER EPIPHANY

O God of wisdom and love, hear and answer our prayers now as we say, Lord in your mercy, hear our prayer.

Bless your church and its leaders, that only your will might guide our witness and that we might be a sanctuary for all people.
Lord in your mercy, **hear our prayer.**

Shower your grace upon our nation. Let our citizenship be guided by your way of love, that our nation's resources might be directed to the welfare and safety of all people.
Lord in your mercy, **hear our prayer.**

Grant us courage and imagination to fulfill our role as stewards of your creation, that our descendants might also know its abundance and beauty.
Lord in your mercy, **hear our prayer.**

Let your law be written on our hearts that we might be agents of love to the world around us, and that our communities might be places where everyone might have the opportunity to live into their potential.
Lord in your mercy, **hear our prayer.**

Make your healing presence known to all who suffer, that they might know wholeness and peace. [Especially we pray for…*prayer list.*]
Lord in your mercy, **hear our prayer.**

Open your arms to the dying, comfort the grieving, and sustain our hope until the day we all might rise in your new age.
Lord in your mercy, **hear our prayer.**

You have shaped and guided your people in the past so that they might be the people you created them to be. Be with us now to show us the pathway to ever deeper relationship with you and your creation, that your love might be made manifest through us. All this we ask through our Lord, Jesus, who with you and the Holy Spirit lives and reigns. **Amen.**

EIGHTH SUNDAY AFTER EPIPHANY

Lord our God grant us the freedom from worldly anxieties and distractions as we open our hearts to you and offer you our heartfelt prayers, saying, Lord in your mercy, hear our prayer.

Lord, we pray for your church that we may be your heart and hands. We pray that we may step outside our own doors to welcome your beloved.
Lord in your mercy, **hear our prayer.**

Lord, we pray for our nation that we might reflect the priorities of your son and welcome the stranger even as we work to improve the lives of all our people. May we be a model nation that values justice, peace, and freedom for every person.
Lord in your mercy, **hear our prayer.**

Lord, we pray for the world, that your people will be at peace, be safe from danger and secure in their family's needs for food and shelter, opportunities, and freedom.
Lord in your mercy, **hear our prayer.**

Lord, we pray for those who long for a better life, for themselves and their children. We ask that you use us to help our brothers and sisters thrive.
Lord in your mercy, **hear our prayer.**

We pray for those who suffer. We pray for those in need. We pray for those who are ill. [Especially for …*prayer list.*]
Lord in your mercy, **hear our prayer.**

Lord, we pray for those who have found peace in you and who reside with you in your eternal kingdom. May light perpetual shine upon them and may that same light give peace to those who grieve.
Lord in your mercy, **hear our prayer.**

We ask this Holy God in the name of your son, who is perfect peace and in the hope of your spirit that reigns with you both. **Amen.**

LAST SUNDAY AFTER EPIPHANY

Holy God, as we wait in expectation for your majesty, we offer you our heartfelt prayers as we say, Lord in your mercy, hear our prayer.

Be present in your church, in the gathering of your people, and send your spirit to enliven and encourage us today.
Lord in your mercy, **hear our prayer.**

We pray for our nation, and for all nations, for those who lead, and for those who work for change, that they may labor to better the lives of their communities.
Lord in your mercy, **hear our prayer.**

We offer our concerns for the earth; for our natural resources and our failures to tend to them. Open our hearts that we might be part of the solution to the problems of the world around us.
Lord in your mercy, **hear our prayer.**

We pray for the people of the earth, for those who hunger, thirst, or yearn for freedom. We pray also for those who have all their needs met, but who are deaf to the cries of the imprisoned, the impoverished, and the persecuted, that their eyes may be opened.
Lord in your mercy, **hear our prayer.**

We long to end the suffering of those in trouble and we ask for your comfort and healing for those who are sick, anxious, hopeless, grieving or dying. Be powerfully present to all those in need. [Especially we pray for… *prayer list.*]
Lord in your mercy, **hear our prayer.**

We pray for the dying and those who gather around them. We pray for a peaceful death and rise in glory in the coming age.
Lord in your mercy, **hear our prayer.**

All this we ask in the certainty of your love, in our longing for your return and in the promise of your coming again. **Amen.**

FIRST SUNDAY IN LENT

God of Wisdom and Mercy, look upon us with compassion; hear and answer our prayers as may be best for us as we say, Lord in your mercy, hear our prayer.

Call your church to repentance for the ways in which we stray from our Lord's example and give us strength to follow him fearlessly and without reservation.
Lord in your mercy, **hear our prayer.**

Let the way of Jesus be an inspiration for all who hold authority in our nation and around the world, that they might desire first the well-being of those they lead and work together to establish peace.
Lord in your mercy, **hear our prayer.**

Grant us an awareness of the temptations that seek to lead us astray that we might amend our lives, and empower us to live into our faith with courage and commitment
Lord in your mercy, **hear our prayer.**

Strengthen us and give us the perseverance and wisdom to care for your creation that we might secure its abundance and diversity.
Lord in your mercy, **hear our prayer.**

Grant your healing presence to all who suffer that they may find wholeness in Christ's love for them.
Lord in your mercy, **hear our prayer.**

Take the dead into your loving care, watch over the grieving with tenderness, and bring us, with all the saints in every generation, into your new age.
Lord in your mercy, **hear our prayer.**

You have promised to be with us when we gather, hear our prayers and be among us. Empower us to do your will and forgive and restore us in our failings. All this we ask through our Lord and redeemer, Jesus Christ, who lives and reigns with you and the Holy Spirit, on God, now and always. **Amen.**

SECOND SUNDAY IN LENT

Heavenly Father, fill all those who lift their hearts to you with a spirit of rebirth, that we might find your joy and pour it out for others in your name. Answer us as we say, Lord in your mercy, hear our prayer.

We pray for the church universal, for our understanding of your holy word to increase and our ability to live the life of service you demand of us to be a source of peace and joy.
Lord in your mercy, **hear our prayer.**

We pray for all nations, that all governments, authorities, and leaders might sacrifice their own desires and power to benefit those with no power. May we become united in our work toward peace, security, and service to the least of these.
Lord in your mercy, **hear our prayer.**

We pray for the world itself, for this earth and all your creation, that we may all work together to repair the harm we have done and to discover new, more sustainable ways of life.
Lord in your mercy, **hear our prayer.**

We pray for those who suffer, for those in trouble and despair, for those who are ill and frightened, for those who are grieving, anxious or hopeless. We pray that those in greatest need may feel you close about them.
[Especially we pray for…*prayer list.*]
Lord in your mercy, **hear our prayer.**

We pray for our own lives and the needs of those we love. We pray for those we do not know and for those we have neglected or harmed. Be mercifully present to us and to all.
Lord in your mercy, **hear our prayer.**

We pray for the departed, for those who are dying and for all those who watch and wait with them. May light perpetual and joy unending be theirs to claims.
Lord in your mercy, **hear our prayer.**

Lord, like Nicodemus we do not fully understand the mysteries of your love and we sometimes willfully ignore the truth of your word. Bring us again into new life lived in you and share with us the joy of your eternal kingdom. To you, to the Son and to the Holy Spirit we pledge our lives. **Amen.**

THIRD SUNDAY IN LENT

God of life, hear the prayers of your people as we say, Lord in your mercy, hear our prayer.

We pray for your church in every guise across the world. Guide us to see what connects us, that the unity of Christ might be made manifest.
Lord in your mercy, **hear our prayer.**

We pray for the nations and their leaders, that they might seek justice, practice mercy, and look always for the welfare and peace of all people.
Lord in your mercy, **hear our prayer.**

We pray for the places we call home, that they might be places of spiritual flourishing and communal harmony.
Lord in your mercy, **hear our prayer.**

We pray for the earth; for the water and soil that sustains us and for our role as stewards of your abundant Creation that we might not despoil it through apathy or greed.
Lord in your mercy, **hear our prayer.**

We pray for all who in serious need or distress; that they might find wholeness in Christ. [Especially we lift up…*prayer list.*]
Lord in your mercy, **hear our prayer.**

We pray for the dead and the dying and for those who grieve; deliver them from their distress grant us all a place in your eternal kingdom.
Lord in your mercy, **hear our prayer.**

God of freedom, God of life hear and answer our prayers as may be best for us and lead us into the place of your promise that we might know abundant life. We ask this in Jesus' name. **Amen.**

FOURTH SUNDAY IN LENT

God of glory, be present as you have promised; hear our prayers and respond swiftly to the yearnings of our hearts as we say, Lord in your mercy, hear our prayer.

Awaken your church to its mission of healing and reconciliation, that it might be a beacon of hope.
Lord in your mercy, **hear our prayer.**

Stir the leaders of this nation to pursue justice and peace so that all who live here might live with dignity and the confidence of a better tomorrow.
Lord in your mercy, **hear our prayer.**

Arouse in us the desire to be engaged with our local communities that they might be places where the potential of all might have a chance to be discovered and nurtured.
Lord in your mercy, **hear our prayer.**

Stir up in us the courage to confront the challenges of a changing climate, that we might ensure a world where future generations might thrive.
Lord in your mercy, **hear our prayer.**

Bring your healing peace to all who suffer and keep us mindful of their needs, that they might know wholeness and healing, resting in the assurance of their beloved-ness.
Lord in your mercy, **hear our prayer.**

Through your Law, your prophets and your Son, O God, you have ever sought to expand our perception and to lead us into deeper relationship with you and your creation. Keep us in your love and show us how might continue Christ's mission of healing and reconciliation in our own lives. All we ask, we ask through Christ, our Lord, who lives and reigns with you and the Holy Spirit, indivisible and forever. **Amen.**

FIFTH SUNDAY IN LENT

Let us pray to the Lord in all humility, yet filled with hope, saying Lord in your mercy, hear our prayer.

Lord God, see to your people and your church; lift up what is good, help us cast aside what is harmful; help us fulfill our call to be Christ in the world today.
Lord in your mercy, **hear our prayer.**

Lord God, guide, and grant wisdom to the leaders of the nations, that they might work cooperatively and for the benefit of all of humanity.
Lord in your mercy, **hear our prayer.**

Lord God, infuse our towns and cities with a spirit of communal well-being, that we might always think first of those who live in the margins and forgotten places; and that where we live might be a place where everyone can thrive and live into their created purpose.
Lord in your mercy, **hear our prayer.**

Lord God, heal what is hurting, mend what is broken, bring to wholeness all who suffer from any distress. [Especially we lift up...*prayer list.*]
Lord in your mercy, **hear our prayer.**

Lord God, help us to preserve the abundance of creation and ensure its sustainable use as you have envisioned for us.
Lord in your mercy, **hear our prayer.**

Lord God, embrace the dead in your loving arms, hold the grieving in your strong hands, and grant us all the new life in your eternal kingdom.
Lord in your mercy, **hear our prayer.**

God of promise, send abundant life into your people, enliven our spirits and lift our hearts through the power of Christ's example through whom we pray. **Amen.**

LECTIONARY YEAR A

SUNDAY OF THE PASSION - PALM SUNDAY

Lord God in humility and reverence we offer you our prayers, be swift to answer them we beg as we say, Lord in your mercy, hear our prayer.

Father, the world waits for your Good News. Be present to all who turn to you, strengthen those who fail or hesitate, come into our lives each day, and give us hearts and greet you with joy.
Lord in your mercy, **hear our prayer.**

We call those who follow you, "the church" – and we have surrounded these faithful people with buildings, ministries, hierarchies, rubrics, headaches, heartaches and deep joy. Remind us that we need only You and one another.
Lord in your mercy, **hear our prayer.**

Give your grace to this nation, to our leaders, to our public servants and to our health care workers and first responders.
Lord in your mercy, **hear our prayer.**

Remind us of just how connected we are and how much we need each other. We offer our deepest prayers for the recovery of the human family, that we might form a sustainable way of life for the well-being of the people of the world.
Lord in your mercy, **hear our prayer.**

Comfort us. Comfort all people. And strengthen us for the days to come. [Especially we pray for…*prayer list.*]
Lord in your mercy, **hear our prayer.**

We mourn those who have died and left this world. Bless the departed with eternal light and joy when the day of new life comes.
Lord in your mercy, **hear our prayer.**

We are entering into a Holy Week stripped bare of its usual patterns and rhythms. Give us the will to use this time to draw closer to you and your Son as we consider the meaning and the unbelievable truth of his passion and death this week, that we might live deeper into the radical offering of love that was the passion of Christ. **Amen.**

MAUNDY THURDAY

Hear us O God as you have promised and respond as may be best for us as we lift our voices in prayer saying: Lord in your mercy, hear our prayer.

May your church be a sacrament to the world, showing forth your love to the world, strengthened by the Holy Spirit, and led by the teachings and example of our Lord, Jesus Christ
Lord in your mercy, **hear our prayer.**

May our nation be blessed with leaders who serve with humility and the desire to work on behalf of all.
Lord in your mercy, **hear our prayer.**

May your creation be healed of the damage we have done and may we be advocates of new and better ways of living that are sustainable and life-giving.
Lord in your mercy, **hear our prayer.**

May your people gathered here be ever mindful of the love of Christ and inspired by his example to embrace his way and be your agents of love in a hurting world.
Lord in your mercy, **hear our prayer.**

May all who know sickness and pain know your healing presence in their lives and be made whole and at peace.
Lord in your mercy, **hear our prayer.**

May the dead be remade through your eternal love and rise again in your new age.
Lord in your mercy, **hear our prayer.**

Through Christ you have gifted us with all we need for the abundant life you have offered. Remember your love for us and lead us ever deeper into relationship with you and with one another, through Christ we pray, who with you and the Holy Spirit are One God, eternal and almighty. **Amen.**

EASTER *Early or Vigil Service*

Alleluia Christ is Risen! Hear our prayers offered this *night/day* from hearts gladdened by the hope of eternal life as we say, Lord in your mercy, hear our prayer.

Grant your church to always hold fast to the example of Christ's life and the hope of His resurrection.
Lord in your mercy, **hear our prayer.**

Fill the hearts of this nation with hope, peace, and a willingness to work together to build a nation where everyone has the opportunity to thrive and to live into their potential.
Lord in your mercy, **hear our prayer.**

Inhabit the lives of all gathered here; be the light that dispels all darkness, vanquishing our fears and giving us the courage to love boldly.
Lord in your mercy, **hear our prayer.**

Fill our hearts with gratitude and thankfulness for the marvelous and abundant diversity of life and empower us to be stewards of your creation that all future generations may glory in all that you have created for us.
Lord in your mercy, **hear our prayer.**

Bring wholeness and healing to all who suffer in body, mind, or spirit, that they might have peace and abundant life.
Lord in your mercy, **hear our prayer.**

We give thanks for the lives of those who have already entered into your glory, and we ask that we too may one day arise in your eternal kingdom.
Lord in your mercy, **hear our prayer.**

Most gracious God, in Christ your love was made manifest in our world, embolden us to courageously continue his ministry and to face without fear where love might take us confident in Christ's promise to stand with us and walk with us always. **Amen.**

EASTER *Principal Service*

Gracious God whose love defeated even death, hear and answer our deepest hopes and needs as you did for the women who discovered the empty tomb and hear our prayers as we say, Lord in your mercy, **hear our prayer.**

Your church is the Body of Christ, constituted and empowered to continue to proclaim Christ's resurrection; strengthen and embolden us to be persistent in our proclamation.
Lord in your mercy, **hear our prayer.**

Our world still falls short of the full blossoming of human potential; open the eyes and hearts of the world's leaders to pursue peace and human thriving for all people.
Lord in your mercy, **hear our prayer.**

Help us to see the risen Christ in the world around; guide us into the work you have given us to do so that the ministries of Jesus might continue; that the world might know his healing and love through our actions.
Lord in your mercy, **hear our prayer.**

You have placed us in a glorious creation and charged us with its care; grant us wisdom and a willingness to protect our environment so that future generations might know the fullness of its beauty and abundance.
Lord in your mercy, **hear our prayer.**

Bring healing and wholeness to our lives and to all who suffer in any way; grant that they might feel Christ's caring touch on their hurts. [Especially we pray for...*prayer list.*]
Lord in your mercy, **hear our prayer.**

Christ's resurrection opened for us the way to eternal life; grant that we all may continue on Christ's pathway and enter into your eternal reign and rise again with all the saints who have gone before.
Lord in your mercy, **hear our prayer.**

Glorious Lord, you have promised to be with us always fulfill now your promises for us and grant our prayers as may be best of us and always in accord with your will. All this we ask through our advocate and redeemer, Christ Jesus who lives with you and the Holy Spirit, eternally one God. **Amen.**

MONDAY IN EASTER WEEK

With gladness of hearts, we make haste to offer you our prayers, Risen Lord, saying Lord in your mercy hear our prayer.

Like our sister Mary of Magdala, we too long to see you, Christ. Open your disciples in this age to the reality of your presence among us and send us anew into the joyful task of shouting out good news.
Lord in your mercy, **hear our prayer.**

May our government and all its leaders embody your care for justice and mercy. May our leaders in towns and counties and cities and capitals rejoice in serving others and may the world stage see an end to the evil of war and a reorientation toward a global goal of peace.
Lord in your mercy, **hear our prayer.**

Open our eyes to see the needs in our own neighborhoods and parishes. Use us to answer prayers and to be a healing presence to those around us.
Lord in your mercy, **hear our prayer.**

Blanket this community with peace and concord. Give us an appreciation for our neighbors and a desire to know them well. Give us your love for the world around us.
Lord in your mercy, **hear our prayer.**

Bless and heal those who are anxious of heart, hopeless in spirit or ill. Give them relief from suffering and a sense of wholeness and peace.
Lord in your mercy, **hear our prayer.**

We pray for the departed with a special care for those who mourn their passing. Welcome them with light and joy into your kingdom.
Lord in your mercy, **hear our prayer.**

With joy in the promises given through Christ's resurrection, these prayers are offered in a spirit of love to you Eternal God, giving thanks to you, your Son, our savior, and the Holy Spirit. **Amen.**

TUESDAY IN EASTER WEEK

We lift up our voices in prayer and supplication, saying Lord in your mercy, hear our prayer.

You have given to your people, the church, the gift of the Holy Spirit to lead us into greater love and greater understanding, grant us the strength to follow.
Lord in your mercy, **hear our prayer.**

Fill the hearts of this world's leaders with a desire to be servants to justice and mercy and to see the dignity of all people, grant us the peace which passes understanding.
Lord in your mercy, **hear our prayer.**

Inspire our imaginations to find ways to undo the damage we have done to the environment and climate, grant us the courage to make bold changes.
Lord in your mercy, **hear our prayer.**

Arouse in us the faith to see in Christ's victory an invitation to abundant life in the here and now. Grant us hearts overflowing with joyous love.
Lord in your mercy, **hear our prayer.**

Let your healing spirit descend upon all who suffer. Grant them release from their pain and fears.
Lord in your mercy, **hear our prayer.**

Welcome the dying, comfort the grieving, and bring us, at the end of our earthly journey into your loving embrace. Grant us all the fulfillment of your promises.
Lord in your mercy, **hear our prayer.**

Through Christ your power entered into the world in new and wondrous ways, enter into our lives that we may know and share your glorious love that transforms all human life. We ask this through the one who has conquered death and opened the pathway to eternal life for all people, this same Christ who with You and the Holy Spirit lives and reigns, forever. **Amen.**

WEDNESDAY IN EASTER WEEK

Risen and holy Savior, we know you in the breaking of bread and the sharing of the cup of your new covenant. As we wait in anticipation for that holy meal, we offer you the crumbs of our hearts as we say Lord in your mercy, hear our prayer

Grant your church a spirit that allows us to take on and tackle projects that will improve our ministry, serve our neighbors and better our own spiritual lives
Lord in your mercy: **hear our prayer.**

Grant our nation a spirit of renewal, revival, and respect for one another and for those who live in different countries and circumstances than we do.
Lord in your mercy: **hear our prayer.**

Give to people in every place those things that are necessary for life – food, shelter, clothing, friends, gratifying work, and meaningful worship of you.
Lord in your mercy: **hear our prayer.**

Grant that all those who feel isolated and alone may turn to a true follower of Jesus and find a place to worship, to grow and to be in community.
Lord in your mercy: **hear our prayer.**

Give to all those who lead or manage others in government, workplaces, homes, and churches the integrity to do what is right, joy in the work they are called to do, and wisdom to avoid temptation.
Lord in your mercy: **hear our prayer.**

Grant healing to those who are sick, suffering or in need
Lord in your mercy: **hear our prayer.**

Give the dying a place at your heavenly banquet and grant them peace at their end.
Lord in your mercy: **hear our prayer.**

These prayers and praises are yours, Almighty Father, who together with your Son and the Holy Spirit, reign this day and always. **Amen.**

THURSDAY IN EASTER WEEK

God of peace, enter in and hear us as we lift up our hopes and needs to you as we say Lord in your mercy, hear our prayer.

That your church may be a non-anxious presence in a world wracked by turmoil and conflict and place of peace and sanctuary for all we pray.
Lord in your mercy, **hear our prayer.**

That this nation may fulfill its promises, offer dignity to all its people, and be an advocate for justice, mercy, and peace in the world we pray.
Lord in your mercy, **hear our prayer.**

That our local community might be a place where children might grow up in peace and security with opportunities to grow into the people they were created to be we pray.
Lord in your mercy, **hear our prayer.**

That this assembly might grow in faith and work together to discern and carry out your mission for us we pray.
Lord in your mercy, **hear our prayer.**

That those impacted by sickness and injury might find relief in your healing love, be returned to wholeness, and know the peace which is beyond comprehension we pray.
Lord in your mercy, **hear our prayer.**

That the dead might be made complete in your love and that we may all rise again together in your new age we pray.
Lord in your mercy, **hear our prayer.**

In Christ you have overcome the darkness which shrouded human life and given us freedom and reason for hope. In thankfulness for your salvation, we offer these prayers through Christ, who with you and the holy Spirit stand over all creation forever. **Amen.**

FRIDAY IN EASTER WEEK

Remembering that Jesus showed love for his friends by sharing food and fellowship, let us pray for the followers of Jesus, for ourselves, and for the world as we say, Lord in your mercy, hear our prayer.

May our hearts and minds be always on you O God. Bless us with silence to hear your voice and share our thoughts with you.
Lord in your mercy: **hear our prayer.**

May our country be a place where children can thrive in their homes, in their families, their schools, and communities. Bless each young life with safety, confidence, and love.
Lord in your mercy: **hear our prayer.**

May our homes be free from anger and division. Bless each of us with patience in our relationships and peace in our households.
Lord in your mercy: **hear our prayer.**

May our communities be places of welcome for those who are not of our faith, our race, our politics, or our preferences. Bless us with the knowing of strangers and angels.
Lord in your mercy: **hear our prayer.**

May our prayers for healing be heard for these friends and acquaintances, that your grace might provide them with restoration.
Lord in your mercy, **hear our prayer.**

May our loved ones depart this life in confidence, without fear. Bless our own leaving with peace and the nearness of loved ones.
Lord in your mercy: **hear our prayer.**

When we are anxious and stray from you, O God. Keep us safely in your hands and hear our prayers for the world and its people. Grant them as may be best for us. In the name of the Father, the Son, and the Holy Spirit. **Amen.**

SATURDAY IN EASTER WEEK

We have gathered to offer you praise and to ask for a response to our hopes and needs; hear us now as pray; Lord in your mercy, hear our prayer.

Let your church be a herald of your Good News and a visible sign of your gracious love to all the world.
Lord in your mercy, **hear our prayer.**

Let our nation be a place of peace and goodwill amongst all people and a positive source of hope for all the world to see.
Lord in your mercy, **hear our prayer.**

Let us learn to be advocates for a peaceful and sustainable future that future generations may know the abundance of creation and call us blessed for our willingness to change.
Lord in your mercy, **hear our prayer.**

Let this assembly know of your presence with us and strengthen us to carry on your work of healing and reconciliation.
Lord in your mercy, **hear our prayer.**

Let all who suffer in any way know release from their pain, their worry, and their fear. Grant them wholeness and hope.
Lord in your mercy, **hear our prayer.**

Let the dying know of your love and of the welcome they will receive into your holy presence, and let all of us see in death the hope won for us through the mighty passion of Christ.
Lord in your mercy, **hear our prayer.**

You have led your people through fear into promise again and again. Through Christ's resurrection give us courage to strive for the promise in our lives. All this we ask through the one who loves us and asks of us our whole selves, Jesus Christ, who with you and the Holy Spirit bestrides creation in this and all ages. **Amen.**

SECOND SUNDAY OF EASTER

Lord God, we are your people, and we confess our need for you in our lives, hear now our prayers as we say Lord in your mercy, hear our prayer.

We pray for your church and all those who follow you and serve the world in your name. May they be strengthened, energized, and comforted by the knowledge of your constant love.
Lord in your mercy, **hear our prayer.**

We pray for those who serve and govern in this nation. May they act wisely with compassion, mercy, and selfless concern for all people.
Lord in your mercy, **hear our prayer.**

We pray for the world, for the sustenance and viability of the earth and its creatures and resources, for the eradication of disease, for the health and livelihood of all people, for those who suffer persecution, homelessness, starvation, imprisonment, and oppression; so that all may be made new.
Lord in your mercy, **hear our prayer.**

We pray for our neighbors, that we might live in peace and safety, that all might have everything they need to live a full and abundant life.
Lord in your mercy, **hear our prayer.**

We pray for the suffering and those in trouble, for those who are anxious and frightened, for those who must face danger as a part of their work in the world. We pray for those who are in hospitals, for those who tend them in their illness. [Especially we pray for…*prayer list.*]
Lord in your mercy, **hear our prayer.**

We pray for the dead and for those who are dying that the love of God might be a strong comfort as they depart this world and for that same comfort to sustain those who mourn.
Lord in your mercy, **hear our prayer.**

You are our strength Lord God, and we gladly lean on you in times of trouble. Take these burdens now and offer us your grace and remind us of your promise that you are always with us. In Jesus' name. **Amen.**

THIRD SUNDAY OF EASTER

God of constant love, be with us now in our times of uncertainty; hear and respond to our prayers as we say Lord in your mercy, hear our prayer.

Grant creativity and persistence to your church and her leaders as it grapples with new ways to be community and finds new avenues and audiences for its message of hope.
Lord in your mercy, **hear our prayer.**

Strengthen the commitment of leaders in our nation, and around the world, to make decisions that prioritize the well-being and sustenance of human life and wellness.
Lord in your mercy, **hear our prayer.**

Help us to be the beacons of hope and agents of love to our neighbors and colleagues.
Lord in your mercy, **hear our prayer.**

Strengthen our resolve to push forward policies that align with your vision of our communal life and our stewardship of the natural world.
Lord in your mercy, **hear our prayer.**

Mend what is broken in our lives and in the world, heal what is sick, make whole what is fractured, bring peace where there is fear or acrimony; make our world whole. [Especially we ask you presence in the lives of… *prayer list.*]
Lord in your mercy, **hear our prayer.**

Welcome the dying into your loving embrace, grant them growth in the knowledge and love of you; care for those who grieve, and welcome us in our turn into the new life promised through Christ.
Lord in your mercy, **hear our prayer.**

Your love for us is a magnificent gift, unearned and undeserved. Lead us to grow in our appreciation and help us to reflect that love into the world around us that we might work hand in hand in building the kingdom of God all around us with Christ, who with you and the Holy Spirit, lives and reigns, One God, now and always. **Amen.**

LECTIONARY YEAR A

FOURTH SUNDAY OF EASTER

Hear us Lord as we lift our voices in common cause saying, Lord in your mercy, hear our prayer.

We pray for the church universal, that the circumstances of this world will lead us into new ways of being the good dream of God; a body of people who love and serve God and neighbor. Lord in your mercy, **hear our prayer.**

We pray for our nation, and all nations, that we might live in health, safety, and peace. We pray for those who govern, that they keep the needs of all people as their first priority; and that truth and mercy are their closest companions.
Lord in your mercy, **hear our prayer.**

We pray for the poor, the hungry and the marginalized and for those whose life's work is to help them with basic needs and the ability to thrive.
Lord in your mercy, **hear our prayer.**

We pray for our unique situations and needs. For health, for the safety and happiness of our families, for our coworkers, friends, neighbors. We pray especially for those things that bring us fear or anxiety, asking that we might shed our concerns and be at peace.
Lord in your mercy, **hear our prayer.**

We pray for those who suffer sickness or debility, that they might know healing and wholeness. [Especially we pray for...*prayer list.*]
Lord in your mercy, **hear our prayer.**

We pray in thanksgiving for this life and, in faith, for the life to come. Bless the dying with your grace and welcome. Grant us also the hope of heavenly reunion in the age to come.
Lord in your mercy, **hear our prayer.**

God of love; you know our needs greater than we know them ourselves; hear us and answer us as you have always done and clothe us in your loving grace that we might fully be your son's continuing work in the world; and all this through Christ, who lives and reigns with you and the Holy Spirit, One God, now and always. **Amen.**

FIFTH SUNDAY OF EASTER

Steadfast God, you have never abandoned your promise to be with your people, be present to us now and hear us as we say, Lord in your mercy, hear our prayer.

Imbue your church with the courage of Stephen, that it may hold steadfast to Christ and uphold always your command to love one another.
Lord in your mercy, **hear our prayer.**

Grant wisdom to those in authority in our lives that they may not be seduced by the expedient or the popular, but strive always to lead us towards true safety, seeking the welfare of all people.
Lord in your mercy, **hear our prayer.**

Embolden us to share our faith with confidence through our actions and choices, and especially in our mercy to those in need.
Lord in your mercy, **hear our prayer**.

Strengthen and sustain us as we forge new ways of life to contend with the conflicts of the world and climate change and help us to hold onto the power of your promises even and especially when we feel hopeless.
Lord in your mercy, **hear our prayer.**

Let your healing presence be known to all who suffer from any trouble; bring wholeness to all that is broken in our lives and in our world.
[Especially we pray for…*prayer list.*]
Lord in your mercy, **hear our prayer.**

Grant peace to the dead and dying, comfort to those who mourn or grieve; let the light of your love dispel the darkness in our hearts.
Lord in your mercy, **hear our prayer.**

Most glorious God, you have strengthened and sustained your people since first you called Abram to follow you. Lift us up, we pray, and help us to be the people we were created to be that we might fulfill your dream for our human family. **Amen.**

SIXTH SUNDAY OF EASTER

Let us pray for the world, saying Lord in your mercy, hear our prayer.
Holy God, through the gift of your spirit we are given the ability to do what you ask of us and the desire to respond with our hearts and hands. Give each person who hears this prayer the ability to live a life of discipleship and the courage to make a difference in the world.
Lord in your mercy, **hear our prayer.**

We pray for the health and welfare of our nation, for the health and security of all nations and for those who have the authority to bring your vision of peace, prosperity, and safety to fruition. Bless us with the will to solve problems, care for the marginalized, and improve the lives of all people.
Lord in your mercy, **hear our prayer.**

We pray for those who are sick and for those who work to heal, that the pain and suffering of this world might be diminished. [We pray especially for…*prayer list.*]
Lord in your mercy, **hear our prayer.**

We pray for those who suffer from abuse, who are not safe at home. We pray for those who have no shelter, for the hungry, the oppressed, the downtrodden and the fearful. We pray for those without hope and who are alone. We pray for those who prey on the weak, for those who seek to do harm and for those who embrace evil – that they might turn away from the darkness inside them and embrace the light of God's love.
Lord in your mercy, **hear our prayer.**

We pray for those who have died, for those whom we remember and long to see. Give us hearts that rest in the hope of a future life lived in your presence.
Lord in your mercy, **hear our prayer.**

Holy God you are our strength and compass. Send us your spirit, your advocate to guide us in this life and strengthen us to love and serve you through service to your people. Be present to us this day and always, as creator, redeemer, and sustainer. **Amen.**

SEVENTH SUNDAY OF EASTER

Lord God who guides us and beckons us ever forward, hear now our prayers as we say, Lord in your mercy, hear our prayer.

Uphold and strengthen your church, reform what is amiss, bolster what is good, and keep us ever mindful of your charge to reflect your love for us into the world.
Lord in your mercy, **hear our prayer.**

Grant wisdom and patience to those in authority in our lives, guide them to always put human life and wellness as their priority.
Lord in your mercy, **hear our prayer.**

Give us courage to be engaged with, and working for, the welfare of our neighbors and the places we call home; help us to see more clearly how to be Christ to one another.
Lord in your mercy, **hear our prayer.**

Open our eyes to the challenges and opportunities in dealing with global issues; give us perseverance and urgency as we develop new and more sustainable ways of being.
Lord in your mercy, **hear our prayer.**

Be present to all who suffer and all who serve them; bring your healing powers to bear and let them know peace and wholeness. [Especially we lift up those who have sought our prayers, for…*prayer list.]*
Lord in your mercy, **hear our prayer.**

Welcome the dying, comfort the grieving, and let the hope of your promises be our consolation and inspiration.
Lord in your mercy, **hear our prayer.**

Loving God, you have given us the example of Christ's life as the template for our own, and you have shown us, in his death and resurrection, the power of your promises to us. Be with us now and always as we strive to live in your kingdom every moment. All this we ask through our Lord and advocate, Jesus the Christ, who lives and reigns with you and the Holy Spirit, one God, now and forever. **Amen.**

PENTECOST

We pray in the power of the spirit this day, asking God to use our hearts and hands to be the Good News to all those we encounter in our lives. We pray that Christ's love will be the lens through which we see the world and the melody of the song we sing, as we respond,
Lord in your mercy, hear our prayer.

Grant us a spirit of reverence for your glory and bless your church, that its worship and work will bring the good news to all who long to hear.
Lord in your mercy, **hear our prayer.**

Lodge the spirit of justice in our hearts and in the hearts of all who hold authority in our lives, that we may all strive for a more perfect human society.
Lord in your mercy, **hear our prayer.**

We pray for the needs of our neighbors, that we might give ourselves wholly to Christ's invitation to walk his way and continue his mission of healing and reconciliation.
Lord in your mercy, **hear our prayer.**

We pray for those who suffer or who are in any need. We pray for the Holy Spirit to give light to the darkness of fear, anxiety, hopelessness and bring release and relief from persecutions.
Lord in your mercy, **hear our prayer.**

We pray for those who have died, for those who are dying and for those who mourn and grieve their passing from this world to the next. Bless the dying with the hope of your eternal kingdom and the grieving with the comfort and healing power of your love.
Lord in your mercy, **hear our prayer.**

Glorious, loving, and creating God; you have never abandoned us and have always offered the lighted path out of our own darkness. Hear and respond to our prayers and may your Holy Spirit blow mightily in our own lives. **Amen.**

TRINITY SUNDAY

Wondrous God, we offer our prayers to you in hope and confidence as we say, Lord in your mercy, hear our prayer.

For the whole church of God, that we might strive for to be as one, as our God is one, that we might fulfill your call to ceaselessly give witness to the power of Christ's example and persevere in continuing his ministry of reconciliation and healing.
Lord in your mercy, **hear our prayer.**

Embolden us to hold our leaders accountable to the possibility of hope and transformation; grant them wisdom and courage to work for the greatest good for all people.
Lord in your mercy, **hear our prayer.**

For the creation, we might be effective stewards and use the abundant resources you have given us wisely and sustainably.
Lord in your mercy, **hear our prayer.**

For this assembly, that we might discern your will for us and deploy the gifts you have given us to build the kingdom of God through our daily lives.
Lord in your mercy, **hear our prayer.**

Bring healing to what is broken in our lives and in the lives of those important to us; help all who suffer that they may find release from their anguish and wholeness in their souls. [Especially we pray for...*prayer list.*]
Lord in your mercy, **hear our prayer.**

Welcome the dying, comfort the grieving, and grant us entry into your eternal presence in the age to come.
Lord in your mercy, **hear our prayer.**

God of mystery, God of love, surround us and fill us with your grace, embolden us to be your agents of love in a hurting world, and answer our prayers as may be best for us and always to your glory. All this we ask through Christ, our Lord. **Amen.**

PROPER 1: *Sunday Closest to May 11*

Let us pray in thanksgiving to God saying, Lord in your mercy, hear our prayer.

Lord our God grant us the freedom from worldly anxieties and distractions as we open our hearts to you and offer you our heartfelt prayers.
Lord in your mercy, hear our prayer.

Lord, we pray for your church that we may be your heart and hands. We pray that we may step outside our own doors to welcome your beloved.
Lord in your mercy, hear our prayer.

Lord, we pray for our nation that we might reflect the priorities of your son and welcome the stranger even as we work to improve the lives of all our people. May we be a nation that values and models justice, peace and freedom for every person.
Lord in your mercy, hear our prayer.

Lord, you created all that we can see and more beyond our comprehension. Give us eyes to see the wonder in all creation, including ourselves. Give us hearts to love all creation and give us the will to strive to be good stewards of the bounty you have given us.
Lord in your mercy, hear our prayer.

Lord, we pray for those who long for a better life, for themselves and their children. We ask that you use us to help our brothers and sisters thrive.
Lord in your mercy, hear our prayer.

We pray for those who suffer and for those in need. We pray for those who are ill. [Especially...*prayer list.*]
Lord in your mercy, hear our prayer.

Lord, we pray for those who have found peace in you and who reside with you in your eternal kingdom. May light perpetual shine upon them and may that same light give peace to those who grieve.
Lord in your mercy, hear our prayer.

We ask this, Holy God, in the name of your Son, who is perfect peace and in the hope of your spirit that reigns with you both to give us strength and purpose. **Amen.**

PROPER 2: *Sunday Closest to May 18*

Creative God, who is our protector, accept our prayers and praises as we lift our voices to you and say, Lord in your mercy, hear our prayer.

Protect your church from error and arrogance, that we might walk humbly and seek only to serve our neighbors.
Lord in your mercy, **hear our prayer.**

Lead our nation away from hateful divisions, that we might celebrate its diversity and create for our neighbors, and for ourselves, a nation of justice, mercy, and peace.
Lord in your mercy, **hear our prayer.**

Grant us wisdom that we might creatively and effectively love and serve our neighbors and build up our communities to be places of hope and opportunity.
Lord in your mercy, **hear our prayer.**

Give us grace and courage to be good stewards of creation, protecting its abundance not only for ourselves but for all the creatures who share its bounty.
Lord in your mercy, **hear our prayer.**

Bring healing and relief to all who know pain, grant them wholeness and peace through the power of your promises. [Especially we lift up… *prayer list.*]
Lord in your mercy, **hear our prayer.**

Open the dwelling places of your love to all who die, that they may know the warmth of your eternal embrace.
Lord in your mercy, **hear our prayer.**

O God, you have fashioned each of us and our world that we might thrive and live into the promise of your creation, shine bright the beacon of hope in our lives that we may always tread the path of Christ. Through the same Christ we pray. **Amen.**

LECTIONARY YEAR A

PROPER 3: *Sunday Closest to May 25*

Lord, you know our hearts and minds, keep our fickle thoughts firmly fixed on you that we might know peace and a growing sense of joy and hear and respond to our prayers as we say; Lord in your mercy, hear our prayer.

Turn our church away from a focus on buildings and budgets and open our needs to the joy of meeting and serving our neighbors and one another. Turn us away from all that keeps us from serving only you that we might attain wisdom and hope.
Lord in your mercy, **hear our prayer.**

Turn our government toward a desire to steward your creation with care and urgency. Turn all nations toward this as well, as we remember the earth was given into our care.
Lord in your mercy, hear our prayer.

Turn our community toward you Lord, that all who hunger for meaning and connection and purpose might find you in this church and in us as we live out our faith.
Lord in your mercy, **hear our prayer.**

Turn our hardships and sufferings into new possibilities for purpose, safety, and vibrant life. Help us to remember that you desire only health and goodness for all of us, and that you make all things new.
Lord in your mercy, **hear our prayer.**

Turn your healing to our brothers and sisters who are sick or in any need of prayer. [Especially for...*prayer list.*]
Lord in your mercy, **hear our prayer.**

Turn the leave-taking of this world into new life with you as we remember all those who have died in faith and who will rise again.
Lord in your mercy, **hear our prayer**

Finally, Lord, turn our prayers into the cadence of our lives. May we never cease to offer you our prayers and petitions and may you never turn away from our heartfelt need to worship and talk to you. In Jesus name, **Amen.**

PROPER 4: *Sunday Closest to June 1*

Wondrous God, full of glory, be present now as you have promised; hear and answer our prayers as may be best for us as we say, Lord in your mercy, hear our prayer.

Bless your church, its mission and ministries, that we may fearlessly and boldly proclaim the good news of Christ through word and deed.
Lord in your mercy, **hear our prayer.**

Bless this nation, grant to all in authority in our lives: wisdom, grace, and humility that they might always seek the greatest good and the welfare of all.
Lord in your mercy, **hear our prayer.**

Bless the places we call home and this place of worship, that your love might be reflected in our lives, blessing all those whom we encounter in our lives.
Lord in your mercy, **hear our prayer.**

Bless those who seek to build a sustainable society in harmony with your creation, that we and all future generations may know its abundance.
Lord in your mercy, **hear our prayer.**

Bless those who suffer with your healing presence, let them know peace and wholeness.
[Especially we pray for…*prayer list.*]
Lord in your mercy, **hear our prayer.**

Bless those who have died and those who stand on the precipice of death, bless those who grieve, and grant to us all an entrance into your eternal presence.
Lord in your mercy, **hear our prayer.**

O Lord, your love for us is unbreakable, let your love give us courage to be your agents of love to shine the brightness of your glory in every shadow that besets us. We ask your strength in the name of Jesus, our Lord and redeemer, who with you and the Holy Spirit reign eternally. **Amen.**

PROPER 5: *Sunday Closest to June 8*

God of patience, you have been steadfast in your love for us, hear us now and answer us as we say Lord in your mercy, hear our prayer.

Bless your church, be our vision that we might follow where you lead, and guard us when we stumble that we might return always to your path.
Lord in your mercy, **hear our prayer.**

Bless the people of this nation and be present with those in authority that they might govern with justice, mercy, and peace and seek always to accomplish the greatest good for all people.
Lord in your mercy, **hear our prayer.**

Bless this assembly that we might be a place of refuge and refreshment; embolden us that we might be advocates for Christ and agents of your love.
Lord in your mercy, **hear our prayer.**

Give us all the foresight and willingness to be effective stewards of your creation, that we might guard its abundance for all future generations.
Lord in your mercy, **hear our prayer.**

Be present to those who suffer, bring healing and wholeness to those who are sick or injured, lift up those who are weighed down by the darkness in the world. [Especially we ask on behalf of those who have sought our prayers; for...*prayer list.*]
Lord in your mercy, **hear our prayer.**

Bless those who have died, welcome them into your eternal care, and grant that we and they may arise again in your new age.
Lord in your mercy, **hear our prayer.**

You have invited us to follow and waited patiently as we have stumbled along your pathway. Continue to be our guide and beacon as we seek to live ever closer to your desire for us. All this we ask in the name of Christ our Lord, who lives with you and the Holy Spirit, One God, now and always. **Amen.**

PROPER 6: *Sunday Closest to June 15*

Holy God, you send us into the world as bearers of your word of peace. Open the hearts of those who receive us, that we might enter into relationship, friendship, and joy with all whom we encounter.
Lord in your mercy, hear our prayer.

We pray for this nation and our government, that each person in authority will search for the words of wisdom and guidance that will lead this nation and all people into safety, health, and justice.
Lord in your mercy, **hear our prayer.**

We pray for the condition of all people and nations, that the Word, revealed to the world, will bring abundant life to all people. We pray for relief for the persecuted, the starving, the diseased, the imprisoned and those who are desperately poor.
Lord in your mercy, **hear our prayer.**

We pray for the needs of our community, for reconciliation and the recognition of the dignity of all persons, for continuing awareness and effective action against the injustice of this world, and for those who have dedicated their lives to the well-being of their neighbors.
Lord in your mercy, **hear our prayer.**

We pray for healing for all who suffer in any way, that they may know wholeness and peace. [Especially we pray for…*prayer list.*]
Lord in your mercy, **hear our prayer.**

We pray for the dying and for their entry into the light of your kingdom, and an awareness that our griefs are not our burden alone.
Lord in your mercy, **hear our prayer.**

Finally, Lord, we pray for your peace to settle on us and remain with us throughout our trials and triumphs. Send us out and give us the courage and the will to live the life you call us toward. Help us to shed our need for preparation and instead inspire us to work boldly to further your kingdom. Bless us this day and always in your name and in the name of your Son and Holy Spirit. **Amen.**

LECTIONARY YEAR A

PROPER 7: *Sunday closest to June 22*

Hear now our prayers most Holy God and throw open the doors of our hearts as we say, Lord in your mercy, hear our prayers.

Guide your church into courageous witness on behalf of Christ, whose example shows us the only path that can lead us away from our fears and hatred and into the glory land of love and reconciliation.
Lord in your mercy, **hear our prayer.**

Grant wisdom to leaders and open their hearts that they might, in confidence and courage, make decisions that lead to mutual flourishing and true peace.
Lord in your mercy, **hear our prayer.**

Open our eyes to injustice in our midst, enliven us so that we may never become numb to the suffering of our neighbors.
Lord in your mercy, **hear our prayer.**

Grant us the perseverance and commitment to make difficult choices and to choose sustainable ways of life that honor your creation, provide safety for all people, and lead us into understanding and reconciliation.
Lord in your mercy, **hear our prayer.**

Be present and bring your healing power to all who suffer in body, mind, or spirit. [Especially we pray for...*prayer list.*]
Lord in your mercy, **hear our prayer.**

Welcome the dying into your loving presence and grant them growth in your love. Comfort the grieving and show us how to honor the legacy of your saints and live into the promise granted us in Christ's death.
Lord in your mercy, **hear our prayer.**

Open our eyes and ears to see your justice unfolding in our midst; grant us wisdom and courage to be agents of your love and fulfill our hopes as may be best for us, but always to your glory. All this we ask through Jesus Christ, our only Lord and redeemer who lives and reigns with you and the Holy Spirit, One God, now and always. **Amen.**

PROPER 8: *Sunday closest to June 29*

Together in loving confidence, we seek your power in our world and in our lives as we say, Lord in your mercy, hear our prayer.

We offer thanksgiving for the church and for all who strive to follow you, finding their strength in the love you have for all people and races. We ask you to be with us in this present age, as we seek justice, peace, and well-being.
Lord in your mercy, **hear our prayer.**

We pray for this nation, for the renewal of its promise; for those elected to serve and all in positions of leadership. We pray also for all those who work for change and the betterment of our institutions.
Lord in your mercy, **hear our prayer.**

We pray for the welfare and the world, for those who work to heal and cure all that ails us.
Lord in your mercy, **hear our prayer.**

We pray for our local community, that all might know health, safety, and opportunity at their most bountiful.
Lord in your mercy, **hear our prayer.**

We pray for those in any kind of need, for those who struggle with hopelessness or anxiety; for those who are homeless, jobless, hungry, or imprisoned.
Lord in your mercy, **hear our prayer.**

We pray for the sick and suffering. [Especially for…*prayer list.*]
Lord in your mercy, **hear our prayer.**

We pray for the dying and for those who mourn that the dying may be brought to kingdom life and the grieving may be brought into the grace of your peace.
Lord in your mercy, **hear our prayer.**

We ask all this with hearts full of love for you, your Son, and the Holy Spirit. **Amen.**

LECTIONARY YEAR A

PROPER 9: *Sunday closest to July 6*

Wondrous and almighty God, you have always desired that we, your creation, might live into the potential you have crafted for us; hear now our prayers and fulfill our desires that we may be wholly and enthusiastically your people as we say, Lord in your mercy, hear our prayer.

Bless your church; give us courage to overcome our divisions, and faith to fulfill our call to bring good news and healing to the world.
Lord in your mercy, **hear our prayer.**

Bless the people of our nation; inspire our very best that we might live into the promise of our founding.
Lord in your mercy, **hear our prayer.**

Bless all the places that are home to us; grant us peace, health, and the true safety that only your grace can bring.
Lord in your mercy, **hear our prayer.**

Bless those whose work supports the healing of our environment and the pursuit of a sustainable way of life.
Lord in your mercy, **hear our prayer.**

Bless those in need of healing and care and bless those whose work supports their welfare. [Especially we lift up…prayer list.]
Lord in your mercy, **hear our prayer.**

Bless those who stand on the threshold of death, grant them a loving welcome and care tenderly with those who grieve their loss.
Lord in your mercy, **hear our prayer.**

God of grace and glory, you have crafted us lovingly in your own image that we might be sustained through relationship with you and one another; make us continually aware of your presence and grant us confidence to reflect your radiant love into the world. All this we ask through our Lord and advocate, Jesus Christ, who with you and the Holy Spirit, lives and reigns, now and always. **Amen.**

PROPER 10: *Sunday closest to July 13*

Heavenly Sower, we offer you grateful hearts for the seeds of faith, mercy, compassion and justice that have been planted in us each season. Give us lives that nurture the good news so that we can share the harvest of your love with others and hear us as we pray Lord in your mercy, hear our prayer.

Give to the church universal the ability to thrive in times of change, help those who are seeking a deeper knowledge of you find a church community that will inspire, support and delight them.
Lord in your mercy, **hear our prayer.**

Bless this nation and all who govern. Bless all nations and all people with health, peace and safety.
Lord in your mercy, **hear our prayer.**

Give us the will to bring peace, justice, and security to all people. Guide us forward that we might end the systems of discrimination and racism so that all your beloved are provided equitable opportunities and safety.
Lord in your mercy, **hear our prayer.**

Comfort those who suffer from abuse, discrimination, disease, anxiety, loneliness, unemployment, homelessness, or hopelessness with your sustaining presence.
Lord in your mercy, **hear our prayer.**

Grant healing to those who are ill from any illness, lead us forward toward a cure and vaccine for the corona virus and protect all those who tirelessly work to heal and care for the sick and suffering. [Especially we pray for... *prayer list.]*
Lord in your mercy, **hear our prayer.**

Deliver the departed into the joy of your kingdom and blanket the grieving with your comfort and peace. Keep us ever mindful that whether we live or whether we die, we are yours and we are loved.
Lord in your mercy, **hear our prayer**

We ask all these things through Jesus Christ, our only strength and advocate. **Amen.**

PROPER 11: Sunday closest to July 20

Almighty God, to know you is joy, to follow your will is true life; hear know our prayers and respond that we might know and follow you more as we pray, Lord in your mercy, hear our prayer.

Inspire your church to be the wellspring of hope for all people; refine and perfect it so that we may be known only for our love.
Lord in your mercy, **hear our prayer.**

Come and dwell in the hearts of our leaders and those with authority in our lives; lead them to desire justice and peace that we might fully live into our liberty and be a beacon of hope to the world.
Lord in your mercy, **hear our prayer.**

Embolden us to be agents of your love in our local community, that it might be a place of promise and possibility where all people might grow and thrive in the light of your grace.
Lord in your mercy, **hear our prayer.**

Enliven our minds that we might creatively, effectively, and sustainably respond to the crises we face, that we might build a way of life that more fully reflects the kingdom of God.
Lord in your mercy, **hear our prayer.**

Mend what is broken, heal what is sick, comfort what is disturbed in our lives and in the lives of all who suffer, that we might know peace and vitality. [Especially we pray for...*prayer list.*]
Lord in your mercy, **hear our prayer.**

Welcome the dying into your love; allow us growth into your kingdom even in death, so that we and all whom we love might one day rise again in your eternal reign.
Lord in your mercy, **hear our prayer.**

All this we ask through Christ, our example, our advocate, and our Lord who stands over all creation and who abides with you and the Holy Spirit now and always. **Amen.**

PROPER 12: *Sunday closest to July 27*

Holy God, be in the midst of us now as we pray for ourselves and the world saying Lord in your mercy, hear our prayer.

We pray for the Church, the body of Christ, that you would be in our midst everywhere we are. Strengthen us, reorient us and send us to be your people to the world.
Lord in your mercy, **hear our prayer.**

We pray for the health, welfare and legacy of this nation. We pray for the prosperity and needs of our brothers and sisters across our country and around the world. Embolden us to serve the common good and advocate for the needs of all people.
Lord in your mercy, **hear our prayer.**

We pray for all creatures on the earth, and for the earth itself. We pray for an end to pollution and the apathy that destroys the creation that you called Good.
Lord in your mercy, **hear our prayer.**

We pray for this congregation, give us hearts that long for you and hands that serve others in your name.
Lord in your mercy, **hear our prayer.**

We pray for those who are sick, suffering, anxious, hopeless, imprisoned, persecuted or alone. We pray for those who are ill and for those who provide them care. [Especially we lift up…*prayer list.]*
Lord in your mercy, **hear our prayer.**

Be with the dying, comfort the grieving and hold us in your heart, this day and always.
Lord in your mercy, **hear our prayer.**

Lord, you have promised to be with us whenever we gather in your name, be with us now. Hear and respond to our prayers. Show us the path to be your people more perfectly. All this we ask in Jesus' name. **Amen.**

LECTIONARY YEAR A

PROPER 13: *Sunday closest to August 3*

Loving and merciful God, hear the prayers of your people as we say Lord in your mercy, hear our prayer.

Lead your church to be a beacon of hope, an advocate of reconciliation, and an example of peace.
Lord in your mercy, **hear our prayer.**

Inspire the leaders of the nations to seek a sustainable and just world where every life has dignity and purpose.
Lord in your mercy, **hear our prayer.**

Fire our hearts that we may shine with zeal for your will and for the mission of Christ our Lord to be good news to our neighbors.
Lord in your mercy, **hear our prayer.**

Strengthen our will and our resolve to work together for sustainable solutions to the issues where only a global effort will suffice.
Lord in your mercy, **hear our prayer.**

Grant peace to all who suffer, mend what is broken, and heal what is sick, so that this world may know the wholeness and goodness of your creation.
[Especially we pray for...*prayer list.*]
Lord in your mercy, **hear our prayer.**

Welcome the dying into your loving presence, be present to those who mourn, and grant us the promise of eternal life.
Lord in your mercy, **hear our prayer.**

Gracious and loving God, whose very being undergirds all of existence. Help us to live into your purpose for us and empower us to be agents of your grace that our lives might reflect your glory. All this we ask through Christ, our redeemer and Lord, who with you and the Holy Spirit lives and reigns now and always. **Amen.**

PROPER 14: *Sunday closest to August 8*

Holy God, you are always with us, in the silence and in the storms. Make us fearless and willing to do your will and hear us as we offer you the deep held prayers of our heart, saying Lord in your mercy, **hear our prayer.**

We pray for the many men and women in every nation who follow Jesus and strive to live his way of Love. Bless the church and send her worshippers into the world to be your hands and heart to all in need. Lord in your mercy, **hear our prayer.**

We pray for this nation and for all who have the responsibility of serving the public good. Bless our public servants with a desire to serve the common good with compassion, generosity, and justice.
Lord in your mercy, **hear our prayer.**

We pray for the needs of the world, for the earth herself, and for the safety and livelihood of all people. Bless us with a deep awareness that our common life is connected; that the welfare of our brother and sister is as important as our own.
Lord in your mercy, **hear our prayer.**

We pray for the health of the world, for doctors, nurses and those called to the vocation of healing and for all those who are afflicted by any illness. Bless those who work to heal, those who wait in hope and those who worry at home. [We pray especially for…*prayer list.*]
Lord in your mercy, **hear our prayer.**

We pray for the dying, for those called from this life into the next, that all might have a place in your kingdom and a deep certainty in your constant presence.
Lord in your mercy, **hear our prayer.**

We offer all these prayers and praises in great hope and certain of your love, through Jesus Christ, our only strength and advocate. **Amen.**

LECTIONARY YEAR A

PROPER 15: *Sunday closest to August 17*

Lord God, let your love dwell within us and shine through our lives that our prayers might lead us into abundant life as we say Lord in your mercy, hear our prayer.

We pray for the church; that it might be a sanctuary and the wellspring of hope for what is broken in our lives and in our world.
Lord in your mercy, **hear our prayer.**

We pray for the nation, that it might live into its promise and be a place of safety, justice, and dignity for all people.
Lord in your mercy, **hear our prayer.**

We pray our local communities, that they might become places inspired by Jesus' vision for human community.
Lord in your mercy, **hear our prayer.**

We pray for our earth; that our land may continue to provide abundantly for our needs and that we might be effective stewards of its riches.
Lord in your mercy, **hear our prayer.**

We pray for those who suffer; that they might be delivered from their distress and know your healing power in their lives. [Especially we pray for *prayer list.*]
Lord in your mercy, **hear our prayer.**

We pray for the dead and the dying; that they might be welcomed into your loving embrace and that they and we might rise again in the glory of your new age.
Lord in your mercy, **hear our prayer.**

God Almighty, creator of all that is, known and unknown; the entirety of your presence and power are beyond our comprehension, help to us understand as best we can and to live lives in accord with your will for us to be laborers for your kingdom. **Amen.**

PROPER 16: *Sunday closest to August 24*

Heavenly Father, through Christ, you came into the world to be truth and life to all who know you. Give us the insight to claim your kingship in our lives and to proclaim this truth to the world as we pray Lord in your mercy, hear our prayer.

We pray for the church, for those who lead worship, for those who pray, for those who prophesy, for those who teach, and for those who serve the world in your name. That together, we might fulfill your mission.
Lord in your mercy, **hear our prayer.**

We pray for this nation; for all in authority and for those who strive to better the lives of all people in our country, that it might be a place of promise and possibility.
Lord in your mercy, **hear our prayer.**

We pray for the welfare of the world; for those who are persecuted and cry for justice; for those who hunger and thirst for knowledge and freedom; for those who work for the common good. That we may know peace and justice in all the world.
Lord in your mercy, **hear our prayer.**

We pray for the needs of our communities, for the hopes of families and for the needs of each of us gathered here. That we might live abundantly.
Lord in your mercy, **hear our prayer.**

We pray for those who suffer, for their relief and comfort and we pray for all who are in need. Asking also that we may be a part of this healing in meaningful ways. [Especially we pray for…*prayer list.*]
Lord in your mercy, **hear our prayer.**

We pray for the dying and the deceased, that all may find a loving home in the kingdom promised to us through our savior. We pray also for those who mourn, that they may be comforted now, in their time of need.
Lord in your mercy, **hear our prayer.**

We offer all these prayers and praises to you O God and ask that they may be granted as may be best for us and for the world. In the name of the Father, Son, and Holy Spirit. **Amen.**

PROPER 17: *Sunday closest to August 31*

Almighty God, you looked upon your people and heard their cries, hear us again and answer us as we pray, Lord in your mercy, **hear our prayer.**

Awaken your church that it might boldly proclaim Christ's good news and continue Christ's mission and ministry throughout the world.
Lord in your mercy, **hear our prayer.**

Guide our nation and those in authority that ours might be a land, not just of promise, but of fulfillment, dignity, and peace.
Lord in your mercy, **hear our prayer.**

Open our eyes to all the opportunities to be your voice and your hands in our local communities so that no needs go unmet.
Lord in your mercy, **hear our prayer.**

Grant us strength, commitment, and perseverance to meet the challenges of our day and to build a sustainable society rooted in our vision of the kingdom.
Lord in your mercy, **hear our prayer.**

Bring healing to all who suffer and mend what is broken or wounded in our lives and in the lives of those we love and care for. [Especially we pray for...*prayer list.*]
Lord in your mercy, **hear our prayer.**

Embrace the dead in your loving arms, grant peace to all who mourn or grieve, and fulfill your promise to us that we might rise again in your new age.
Lord in your mercy, **hear our prayer.**

We cannot know your full glory, and yet you have shown us again and again, inviting us into ever-deepening relationship as your people. Continue to lead us and to answer our prayer as may be best for us and always to your glory. Through Christ our Lord who with you and the Holy Spirit stands supreme throughout creation and beyond, now and always. **Amen.**

PROPER 18: *Sunday closest to September 7*

Almighty God, you are present with us always and you champion those who work to heal our differences. Be with us now as we open our hearts in humility and love to pray for ourselves and the world saying, Lord in your mercy, hear our prayer.

We are your church, bearers of your message of love and hope. Give us voices to invite and welcome our neighbors into their place in your church and grant us humility to face the opportunities we have missed and the mistakes we have with repentance and a desire to make amends.
Lord in your mercy, **hear our prayer.**

We are a nation that cries out to you for healing and peace. Bring us out of division and into relationship. Bless us with leaders who care deeply for the needs of all people and public servants who find joy in reconciliation and justice.
Lord in your mercy, **hear our prayer.**

Bless each person in our local community life with health and safety. Give us new ways of conserving resources, feeding the hungry and working together for the common global good.
Lord in your mercy, **hear our prayer.**

We pray for those who face danger or oppression; for those who are anxious and feeling separate from their neighbors; for those who have nowhere to turn and who are alone. Send us into the midst of those who need your love that we might be the bearers of your healing love. Send your love into the midst of our own being so that we might remember that you are with us always.
Lord in your mercy, **hear our prayer.**

We pray for those who suffer in body, mind, or spirit. [Especially we pray for...*prayer list.*]
Lord in your mercy, **hear our prayer.**

We are but flesh, and our days are numbered. Be present with those who are dying and comfort all those who grieve this day. Bring us into the reconciliation and restoration of kingdom life here and in the world to come.
Lord in your mercy, **hear our prayer.**
God of hope, you have always stood by your people and fulfilled your promises to them; stand with us now and answer our prayer as may be best for us and always to the fulfillment of your dreams and hopes for us; through Christ our Lord, who lives and reigns with you and the Holy Spirit, One God, now and always. **Amen.**

PROPER 19: *Sunday closest to September 14*

Almighty Deliverer, you have heard and lifted up your people again and again; hear us now as we pray saying Lord in your mercy, hear our prayer.

Grant your church wisdom in discerning your call to us that we might be the beacon of hope you have intended us to be.
Lord in your mercy, **hear our prayer.**

Give us courage and determination in our civic life, that we might be witness to the power of repentance, reconciliation, and justice to our neighbors.
Lord in your mercy, **hear our prayer.**

Lead us into a way of life that is sustainable and equitable, that all might participate in the bounty of your creation.
Lord in your mercy, **hear our prayer.**

Open our eyes, our hearts, and our hands to respond to the needs of those around us who suffer from the lack of basic needs; show us how to respond in love to the wants we encounter.
Lord in your mercy, **hear our prayer.**

Bring healing and wholeness to all who suffer, who face illness, or who are wounded; mend what has broken in our lives. [Especially we pray for… *prayer list.*]
Lord in your mercy, hear our prayer.

Embrace the dying in your grace, grant them and us new life in the kingdom to come.
Lord in your mercy, **hear our prayer.**

Sovereign Lord, grant us deeper understanding and love of you, that we might grow to the stature you intended for us and answer our prayers through Christ, our only Lord, who lives with you and the Holy Spirit, One God, now and always. **Amen.**

PROPER 20: *Sunday closest to September 21*

Almighty God, keep us ever mindful of your role in our lives and lead us into the generosity, compassion, and fulfillment of your kingdom as we pray for ourselves and the world, as we say Lord in your mercy, hear our prayer.

Give all congregations, churches, and houses of worship the desire to be generous in time, talent and treasure and especially in forgiveness.
Lord in your mercy, **hear our prayer.**

Give this nation eyes that are open to the truth that your ways are more loving and merciful than ours and create generations of leaders and servants who will strive to bring this lens to how we act in the world and with each other.
Lord in your mercy, **hear our prayer.**

Give each person a calling to live life in a way that brings joy and peace to others; that that same joy and peace may be reflected in our own hearts and souls.
Lord in your mercy, **hear our prayer.**

Give courage and strength to those who advocate for others, work to cure or stand for justice. Bless our world with the spirit of your love and the vision of your kingdom.
Lord in your mercy, **hear our prayer.**

Give healing and peace to those who are ill, anxious, imprisoned, alone or in despair. [Especially we pray for… *prayer list.*]
Lord in your mercy, **hear our prayer.**

Give hope to the dying for the kingdom life that is to come, comfort those who grieve loss and restore relationships to those now separated, whatever the reason.
Lord in your mercy, **hear our prayer.**

All this we ask in the name of your embodied love, Jesus the Christ, our only strength, and advocate, who lives and reigns with you and the Holy Spirit, one God forever. **Amen.**

LECTIONARY YEAR A

PROPER 21: *Sunday closest to September 28*

Almighty God, hear the prayers of your people and come swiftly to aid us as we say, Lord in your mercy, hear our prayer.

Grant your church wisdom to bring about the beloved community through our commitment to individual and communal transformation and redemption.
Lord in your mercy, **hear our prayer.**

Grant our nation strength and forbearance to peacefully resolve our differences and to live in amity with our neighbors.
Lord in your mercy, **hear our prayer.**

Grant an abiding faith and discerning hearts to all of us gathered to hear these words; that we might live into your will and be your people.
Lord in your mercy, **hear our prayer.**

Give to us clarity, that we might perceive and comprehend the gravity of the global issues which we face, and a determination to work together to implement sustainable and equitable solutions.
Lord in your mercy, **hear our prayer.**

Lift the burdens of those who are ill, those who face overwhelming challenges, and those who are fearful. Bring them healing and peace.
[Especially we pray for… *prayer list.*]
Lord in your mercy, **hear our prayer.**

Grant peace and a welcome into your eternal grace to those who have died; and bring us to that place where with them we may all live again in your glorious kingdom.
Lord in your mercy, **hear our prayer.**

God of power and might, your eternal essence is love. Guide us as we seek to live fully into our belovedness and grant us an answer to our prayers that fulfills our deepest longings and reflects your glory into the darkness of our lives and world. All this we ask through your Son, our Lord, who with you and the Holy Spirit reigns supreme, One God, indivisible, forever and ever. **Amen.**

PROPER 22: *Sunday closest to October 5*

Holy God, you call us to be your people and to live in ways that honor you and all people. Give us hearts that cleave to your command to love you and to love our neighbor as much or more than we love ourselves. Hear us as we pray, Lord in your mercy, hear our prayer.

We pray for the church, in the world at this time; that we might be Christ's hands and feet in a world that still cries for deliverance.
Lord in your mercy, **hear our prayer.**

We pray for our nation, for the health, safety, and peace of all people everywhere.
Lord in your mercy, **hear our prayer.**

We pray for the needs of the world; for an end to warfare; for the recognition of rights for all people; and for those who are persecuted, that they may be set free from the bonds of oppression and despair.
Lord in your mercy, **hear our prayer.**

We pray for all those affected by disaster, both natural and human caused, that we might find ways to make positive changes for the benefit of all.
Lord in your mercy, **hear our prayer.**

We pray for those who suffer from illness, anxiety, depression, loneliness, grief, or hopelessness, that their burdens might be lightened by our compassion and your love. [Especially we pray for... *prayer list.*]
Lord in your mercy, **hear our prayer.**

We remember and offer to you our prayers for the dead, that they might celebrate new life in your kingdom, in your eternal presence.
Lord in your mercy, **hear our prayer.**

All this we ask in love, through You, your Son, and the Holy Spirit. **Amen.**

PROPER 23: *Sunday closest to October 12*

Lord God, we lift our hopes and desires to you as we pray, Lord in your mercy, hear our prayer.

Be with your church; move it towards righteousness; lead it to unity in purpose and mission, and guard it from all evils.
Lord in your mercy, **hear our prayer.**

Care for this nation and its people, grant us courage to face up to the ways we fall short of its promises and show us how to work together to increase liberty and dignity for all who live here.
Lord in your mercy, **hear our prayer.**

Deepen our commitment to our neighbors and open our eyes, and hearts, and hands to those in need that we might continue Christ's work among them.
Lord in your mercy, **hear our prayer.**

Energize us for the work of creation care, that we and all future generations might experience fully the abundance of the world you created and placed us in.
Lord in your mercy, **hear our prayer.**

Fulfill the longing for healing and peace to all who suffer in any way; mend what is broken in our lives and in the lives of those we love. [Especially we pray for… *prayer list.]*
Lord in your mercy, **hear our prayer.**

Give rest to those who have died, let them grow in your love, and deliver them and us into the resurrection of your new age.
Lord in your mercy, **hear our prayer.**

Holy God, who knows our needs and wants better than we know ourselves, be with your people and sustain us with your promises that we might participate in your salvation. All this we ask through Jesus, your son and our Lord, who lives and reigns with you and the Holy Spirit, One God now and always. **Amen.**

PROPER 24: *Sunday closest to October 19*

Lord, you call us to give to you those things that belong to you. Give us such an awareness of your presence that we might respond with generosity to the needs of those who call upon you. Hear us as we pray, Lord in your mercy, hear our prayer.

We pray for the people of God throughout the world, help us to find unity in mission and to recognize your wondrous diversity in our differences. Lead us ever deeper into relationship with you.
Lord in your mercy, **hear our prayer.**

We pray for the needs of our country, that elected officials and civil servants may work with integrity. We pray also for the neediest among us who need relief that only our common action can provide. Help us to find common purpose.
Lord in your mercy, **hear our prayer.**

We pray for the needs of the world, especially for those who experience violence, disasters, oppression, and endemic poverty. Help us to respond to the needs we see with personal discipline and generous giving.
Lord in your mercy, **hear our prayer.**

We pray for the places where we live, work, and learn. Bless our communities and families with good health, and the resources to adequately meet all our needs. Make us grateful for what we have and passionate about the needs of our neighbors.
Lord in your mercy, **hear our prayer.**

We pray for those who suffer from illness, anxiety, homelessness, guilt, shame, or apathy. Give strength and healing to all who are in need and give us compassion when we see the afflictions of others. Make us concerned for the welfare of all people. [Especially we pray for... *prayer list.*]
Lord in your mercy, **hear our prayer.**

We pray for the departed, especially for those who have died needlessly and alone, for those who died too soon, and for those who died at the hands of others. Make us aware of the preciousness of life.
Lord in your mercy, **hear our prayer.**

We pray these things in humility acknowledging that we often fail in the very things we ask of you. Give us courage and a willingness to change. Make us the instruments of your reign in this life and always. In Jesus' name. **Amen.**

PROPER 25: *Sunday closest to October 26*

God of deliverance, hear our prayers and deliver us into your kingdom as we say, Lord in your mercy, hear our prayer.

Deliver your church from arrogance and fear; lead us into the places you wish us to go and into the work you wish us to do.
Lord in your mercy, **hear our prayer.**

Deliver this nation from division and anger; bend our hearts that, united, we might work towards justice and dignity for all people.
Lord in your mercy, **hear our prayer.**

Deliver our world from indifference to the welfare of others as we negotiate new ways of being to overcome our global challenges.
Lord in your mercy, **hear our prayer.**

Deliver all of us who hear these words from indecision and doubt, that we might boldly take up Christ's work of healing and reconciliation as our own.
Lord in your mercy, **hear our prayer.**

Deliver all who suffer from their distress and grant them peace and a sense of well-being. [Especially we pray for… *prayer list*].
Lord in your mercy, **hear our prayer.**

Deliver the dead into your eternal kingdom, comfort those who grieve with the hope of reuniting again one day in the resurrection.
Lord in your mercy, **hear our prayer.**

Loving God who time and again has heard your people's cry and lifted them from their despair, hear our prayers and lift us up that we might, more fully, be the people you created us to be and empower us for your mission of love. We ask this in Jesus' name. **Amen.**

PROPER 26: *Sunday closest to November 2*

Holy One, we are your students, learning what love and mercy are from the words and examples of Jesus. We call out to you as children seeking your comfort and praise as we prayerfully say Lord in your mercy, hear our prayer.

Lead us, as your church, to practice what you teach with our lives; that we might draw others to you by our example.
Lord in your mercy, **hear our prayer.**

Lead our nation in the ways of righteousness and peace. Make us champions of goodness and servants of the people, in all areas of government large and small.
Lord in your mercy, **hear our prayer.**

Lead our communities to seek new ways of service and new partnerships that serve those most in need; the homeless, the working poor, the lonely, the elderly, the addicted, the young, the desperate and those whose needs are known to you alone.
Lord in your mercy, **hear our prayer.**

Lead the nations of the world to find new ways to feed the hungry and new methods of insuring peace.
Lord in your mercy, **hear our prayer.**

Lead the sick and suffering to seek your healing love and bless them with relief in body, mind and spirit. [We pray especially for…*prayer list*].
Lord in your mercy, **hear our prayer.**

Lead those who die in this world into life in the next. May light perpetual shine upon them and angels greet them as they enter kingdom life.
Lord in your mercy, **hear our prayer.**

Make us such true followers in faith that we hunger to address all things that we pray for this day and always, most merciful father, in the power of your spirit and the name of your son. **Amen.**

LECTIONARY YEAR A

PROPER 27: *Sunday closest to November 9*

God of promises, we praise your glory and majesty as we humbly offer, from our hearts, prayers for your presence in our lives as we say Lord in your mercy hear our prayer.

Uphold and strengthen your church; show us how to be salve to a wounded world and a place of hope and aspiration amidst despair and cynicism.
Lord in your mercy, **hear our prayer.**

Grant our nation a spirit of cooperation; grant our elected leaders the wisdom and courage to do what is right and grant us and our fellow citizens a renewed commitment to liberty and community.
Lord in your mercy, **hear our prayer.**

Let each of us be agents of healing and reconciliation in the places we call home; that our love for you shines forth in all we do.
Lord in your mercy, **hear our prayer.**

Unite the people of the world to address our global challenges and give us the fortitude to make and hold difficult choices.
Lord in your mercy, **hear our prayer.**

Bring healing and wholeness to all who suffer so that they might experience and know the peace which passes understanding that only you can offer. [Especially we pray for…*prayer list*].
Lord in your mercy, **hear our prayer.**

Remember the dead and bring us together with them in your coming kingdom.
Lord in your mercy, **hear our prayer.**

We give thanks for your love and steadfast promises; grant us lives worthy of the gift of your grace and answer our prayers to our benefit and to your glory. Through Jesus Christ, who lives and loves with you and the Holy Spirit eternally. **Amen.**

PROPER 28: *Sunday closest to November 16*

Lord, you give us the gift of life and call us to use this gift for the betterment of the world and the glory of your name. Grant us courage to use your gift fearlessly and in joy and hear us as we say, Lord in your mercy hear our prayer.

We pray for the church to be in deeper relationship with each community, for the wisdom to reach those who hunger for you, and to bring them into the work of loving and serving the world in your name.
Lord in your mercy, **hear our prayer.**

We pray for this nation and all nations. We pray for the life and needs of all people and an end to policies of oppression. We pray for those who govern, that they might have hearts for their people and priorities for those most in need.
Lord in your mercy, **hear our prayer.**

We pray for our local community and this congregation, that we might cling to hope and labor ceaselessly to build the kingdom in our midst.
Lord in your mercy, **hear our prayer.**

We pray for the health of the world, for sustainable policies that ensure the abundance of creation and the thriving of people and all your creatures.
Lord in your mercy, **hear our prayer.**

We pray for an end to illness and suffering. We pray for those who work to bring hope, healing and assistance to those who are lost, marginalized, imprisoned, ill, suffering, persecuted or broken. [Especially we pray for… *prayer list*].
Lord in your mercy, **hear our prayer.**

We pray for the promise of new life and for all those who are leave this life with the hope of being in your presence. May we and all those who came before and who will come after us, enter into your kingdom to hear your praise: "Well done good and faithful servant."
Lord in your mercy, **hear our prayer.**

Lord, hear these prayers and answer them as may be best for us, O Father, O Son and Holy Spirit. **Amen.**

PROPER 29: CHRIST THE KING *Sunday closest to November 23*

Lord Christ, we offer our selves to your service and love; hear these prayers offered now in your name as we say, Lord in your mercy, hear our prayer.

The assembly of God's people, the Church, are your hands and feet in this world; grant us courage and wisdom as we seek to continue your mission in the world.
Lord in your mercy, **hear our prayer.**

Endow our nation with your peace and embolden us to bring the light of your love to our neighbors, that we might dispel the darkness of fear and hatred.
Lord in your mercy, **hear our prayer.**

Open our eyes, our hearts, and our hands to see and respond to the needs of our neighbors; and to respond with joy and energy so that your love is made manifest in their lives.
Lord in your mercy, **hear our prayer.**

Grant us the spirits of wisdom, curiosity, and persistence, as we seek to weave sustainable practices into our lives; that we might better protect and preserve the bountiful abundance of your creation.
Lord in your mercy, **hear our prayer.**

Deliver us from fear and anxiety, that we might be healers; bring to wholeness all that is broken, and grant peace and deliverance to all who suffer. [Especially we pray for *prayer list*].
Lord in your mercy, **hear our prayer.**

Welcome the dying into your arms, envelop the grieving with your strength, and lift the dread of death from our hearts by increasing our faith and securing our hope in your promises.
Lord in your mercy, **hear our prayer.**

Christ our king and only Lord, we offer you ourselves: our very souls and bodies; that we might participate in the building of your kingdom in our lives and in the world; and we offer you our praise and glory; hosanna in the highest! In Jesus name. **Amen.**

Lectionary Year B

FIRST SUNDAY OF ADVENT

God of anticipation, listen and respond as we raise our voices in prayer, saying, Lord in your mercy, hear our prayer.

For your church that it may be a herald of the age to come and a bastion of hope in the world today.
Lord in your mercy, **hear our prayer.**

For leaders in our civic and communal lives, that they might look beyond the quarrels of today to lay the foundations of justice and mercy for tomorrow,
Lord in your mercy, **hear our prayer.**

For this congregation, that we might rest in your promises as we prepare ourselves for the work of being the body of Christ in the world.
Lord in your mercy, **hear our prayer.**

For our environment, that it might be restored and sustained that its life-giving abundance might be preserved.
Lord in your mercy, **hear our prayer.**

For the sick, the suffering, the anxious, the despairing, and for all in need of your healing presence, that wholeness, reconciliation, and peace might be theirs. [Especially for those who have sought our prayers, for… prayer list].
Lord in your mercy, **hear our prayer.**

For those who have died, and those who are dying, that through the power of your promises they may come to know the joy of your eternal presence.
Lord in your mercy, hear our prayer.

As we enter this time of waiting, strengthen and enliven our faith that we may know the joy of your presence and that our lives might be a reflection of your glory. All these we ask through Jesus, the light of our lives. **Amen.**

SECOND SUNDAY OF ADVENT

Lord God, you proclaim comfort for your people and sent your only son to embody that love. Give us hearts ready to prepare a way for you that we may be a strong word of faith to the world in your name as we pray: Lord in your mercy, hear our prayer

Comfort your church with the good news that Jesus came on earth to live among us, heal us and set us free. Help us to share that good news with others.
Lord in your mercy, **hear our prayer.**

Comfort this nation with a spirit of compassion and justice for the poor and lowly. Help us to give from our abundance and even from our scarcity.
Lord in your mercy, **hear our prayer.**

Comfort the world with your promise of peace and help us to be peace makers and advocates for all who are oppressed, all who are hungry and alone, all who have been abandoned and marginalized.
Lord in your mercy, **hear our prayer.**

Comfort the sick with your healing grace, that they may no peace and release from the burdens of fear, anxiety, and pain. [Especially we pray for...*prayer list*].
Lord in your mercy, **hear our prayer.**

Comfort the dying and the grieving Lord with the promise of life eternal. Help us to stay strong even in the face of loss.
Lord in your mercy, **hear our prayer**

We ask all this in sure confidence that you hear our prayers and will do all that is best for us. Thank you, Holy God, Father, Son and Holy Spirit. **Amen.**

THIRD SUNDAY OF ADVENT

Marvelous and magnificent God, we praise you and proclaim your power in our prayers as we say Lord in your mercy hear our prayer.

Inspire your people to have the confidence of Mary in their proclamation of your Good News. Give us words to sing.
Lord in your mercy, **hear our prayer.**

Rouse those in authority in our lives to exercise their power with mercy and grace, with their eyes on the goals of justice and peace. Give them wisdom.
Lord in your mercy, **hear our prayer.**

Energize this assembly to perceive the opportunities of mission and evangelism in our neighborhood that Christ may be truly known through us. Give us grace.
Lord in your mercy, **hear our prayer.**

Galvanize your people to be stewards of creation, building commitment and trust that we might find sustainable solutions to our climate and environmental challenges. Give us patience.
Lord in your mercy, **hear our prayer.**

Unleash your healing power in the lives of all who suffer, bring them healing and wholeness. Give them peace. [Especially we pray for… *prayer list*].
Lord in your mercy, **hear our prayer.**

Keep those who have died in your eternal love, grant us entry into your presence when we cross that threshold of death, and grant the comforts of faith to those who grieve. Give us all your salvation.
Lord in your mercy, **hear our prayer.**

Through your prophets you have proclaimed your glorious presence in the world. Grant us the power and courage to continue their proclamations in our sharing of the gospel through word and action. All we ask and desire, we do through the one who was and is and is to come, Christ, our Lord and redeemer. **Amen.**

FOURTH SUNDAY OF ADVENT

Heavenly father you look with favor upon all those who find themselves in lowly states and you welcome those who worship you in truth and love. Hear our prayers as we say Lord in your mercy, hear our prayer.

Bless the church Lord, in all its imperfections as it strives to live out your steadfast love to those in the pews and those outside our doors.
Lord in your mercy, **hear our prayer.**

Bless this nation with peace, prosperity, passion for the needs of others and joy in the abundance we have been given. Give our leaders hearts that sing for the needs of all people and all places.
Lord in your mercy, **hear our prayer.**

The world waits for good news and hungers for ways to work together. Give us the right words and ideas to make this world a place that is fit for the coming of your son.
Lord in your mercy, **hear our prayer.**

Many of our friends and family are ill and hurting; many in our community need your help with anxiety, depression, disease, dislocation, and anger. Bless our town and all towns with your healing grace. [We pray especially for…*prayer list*].
Lord in your mercy, **hear our prayer.**

Comfort the dying with the promise of your Son who conquered death on our behalf. Bless the grieving with the sure faith that death is an entrance to new life in you.
Lord in your mercy, **hear our prayer.**

May these prayers be welcome in your heart and may we be used by you to bring the prayers of others into fruition. In the name of the Father, the Son and the Holy Spirit. **Amen.**

FIRST SUNDAY AFTER CHRISTMAS

God of Joy, basking in the love shown to us through the Incarnation of Christ, we lift our hearts to you in devotion and gratitude as we say, Lord in your mercy, hear our prayer.

Fill your church with rejoicing at Christ's presence and make it a place of welcome to all people.
Lord in your mercy, **hear our prayer.**

Let the leaders of our nation be guided by your wisdom, let us and those we name as enemies be reconciled, and may your peace be known across the world.
Lord in your mercy, **hear our prayer.**

Let our worship today strengthen our faith and give us the will and desire to carry out the gospel mission entrusted to us.
Lord in your mercy, **hear our prayer.**

Imbue our souls with awe and wonder in contemplation of your Creation and show us how to be effective stewards of its beauty and abundance.
Lord in your mercy, **hear our prayer.**

Mend what is broken, fill what is emptied, and make whole what has been diminished in our lives and in the lives of our neighbors. [Especially we pray for...*prayer list.*]
Lord in your mercy, **hear our prayer.**

Enfold the dead and dying into your loving embrace, grant them the promise of eternal life made manifest through Jesus, and allow us entry into your new age at the end of our mortal journey.
Lord in your mercy, **hear our prayer.**

Your Christ entered the world from an unexpected place, expand our perspective that we might discern the presence of Christ in the unexpected people and places of our own lives, that we may more perfectly reflect your glory. All this we ask through Christ, who with you and the Holy Spirit lives reigns forever and ever. **Amen.**

SECOND SUNDAY AFTER CHRISTMAS

The word of God lives among and within us to strengthen and inspire. With confidence let us pray to our God with words of hope and faith, saying Lord in your mercy, hear our prayer.

Let us pray for the church of Jesus Christ:
God of light, empower your ministries and people to proclaim your gospel fearlessly wherever darkness obscures human dignity.
Lord in your mercy, **hear our prayer.**

Let us pray for the nations of this world:

God of peace, in your word we recognize the abundance of your enduring love. Grant to this world, marked by division and strife, a thirst for justice perfected in selfless love.
Lord in your mercy, **hear our prayer.**

Let us pray for all educators:
God of wisdom, in your word we hear the proclamation of your truth. Enlighten all who teach with your Spirit of knowledge and understanding.
Lord in your mercy, **hear our prayer.**

Let us pray for this community of faith:
God of grace, give us hearts filled with love, voices to speak your praise, and lives conformed to the image of your Son.
Lord in your mercy, **hear our prayer.**

Let us pray for those who are suffering:
God of glory, in your word we receive the promise of life beyond weakness and sorrow. Heal those who call upon you in faith and reveal your light to those in the shadow of death. [We especially remember those on our prayer list.]
Lord in your mercy, **hear our prayer.**

Let us pray for those who have died:
God of promises, receive the departed into your eternal care and grant that they and we may meet again in your new age.
Lord in your mercy, **hear our prayer.**

Creator of all, you have not abandoned your creation, but have made your dwelling with us in Christ. Hear your faithful people, and grant us the blessings of your mercy, for we make this prayer in the name of Jesus who is Lord forever and ever. **Amen.**

FIRST SUNDAY AFTER THE EPIPHANY: THE BAPTISM OF OUR LORD

Bright Light of the Universe, you declared your intent that the world should not be in darkness and created light. Let that light illumine our hearts as we pray Lord in your mercy, hear our prayers.

That your church might be a beacon that draws all people to Your Son. That many will hear the invitation that is your baptism and respond with Yes.
Lord in your mercy, **hear our prayer.**

That this nation might light the darkness of its people with leadership that opens doors for people in need and shuts out the grasping evil of greed and indifference.
Lord in your mercy, **hear our prayer.**

That our community might experience a revival of faith and love for You and for one another.
Lord in your mercy, **hear our prayer.**

That each person here will experience a deep and enlightening knowledge of Jesus and turn from the shadows we harbor in our hearts and lives.
Lord in your mercy, **hear our prayer.**

That the suffering know your healing love and that we will pray daily for their peace and strength. [We pray especially for...*prayer list*.]
Lord in your mercy, **hear our prayer.**

That the dying will enjoy the epiphany of homecoming in your kingdom and that light perpetual will shine upon them.
Lord in your mercy, **hear our prayer.**

Glorious God, through your beloved Son, you have shown us the path of redemption and the course of abundant life. Continue to call out to us, let your bright and shining love be the beacon that draws further into your kingdom. **Amen.**

SECOND SUNDAY AFTER THE EPIPHANY

We come before you O God lifting our hearts and voices in in the confident hope of your reply as we say, Lord in your mercy, hear our prayer.

Help your people to overcome their divisions that we might work together to further the gospel mission to a world in need of mercy, hope, and justice.
Lord in your mercy, **hear our prayer.**

Embolden us to hold our leaders accountable for building a just and equitable society where no one's basic needs go unmet, and everyone's dignity is respected.
Lord in your mercy, **hear our prayer.**

Strengthen this congregation and be our shepherd that we might joyfully and effectively be Christ to our neighbors.
Lord in your mercy, **hear our prayer.**

Keep us ever mindful of our responsibilities as the caretakers and keepers of your Creation and let us be creative and bold in responding to our environmental challenges.
Lord in your mercy, **hear our prayer.**

Bring those who suffer into your healing embrace so that they may know peace and wholeness and strengthen those who are caretakers and healers for the trials they will face. [Especially we pray for...*prayer list*.]

Lord in your mercy, **hear our prayer.**

Welcome the dying into your presence that your will for them may be complete and grant us entry into that heavenly country where pain and death are no more.
Lord in your mercy, **hear our prayer.**

O God, you have illumined your people with grace, love, and mercy. Help us to be the people you created us to be that our lives might more fully reflect the good news of Jesus and our world transformed through our loving action. We offer our prayers in the name of Jesus, who is the light that guides us. **Amen.**

LECTIONARY YEAR B

THIRD SUNDAY AFTER THE EPIPHANY

Lord God, you call us to repent of our sins and believe in good news. Give us the strength to obey, as we pray; Lord in your mercy, **hear our prayer.**

You ask the church to be your heart and hands and feet in the world. Give us the desire to be your love in the world.
Lord in your mercy, **hear our prayer.**

Your church is wonderful in its diversity. Bless our church and diocese, our priests and deacons, our lay leaders and faithful worshipers.
Lord in your mercy, **hear our prayer.**

You give us pride in our nation and resources. Give us the will to share our abundance with those in need, both near and far.
Lord in your mercy, **hear our prayer.**

You give us your gifts and the created world to serve. Give us the way forward to just stewardship of this planet and all its creatures.
Lord in your mercy, **hear our prayer.**

You give us the gift of faith and healing. Give us the grace to pray deeply for those in greatest need, especially the sick. [We pray especially for… *prayer list.*]
Lord in your mercy, **hear our prayer.**

You give us the promise of abiding with you when we die; keep your promises and give us faith to know you and to trust in them.
Lord in your mercy, **hear our prayer.**

O Most Holy One, you give to us love and mercy, not by our merits, but by your hopes for each of us. Give us a life lived in worship of you, in thanksgiving for your Son, and in fellowship with your Holy Spirit this day and always. **Amen.**

FOURTH SUNDAY AFTER THE EPIPHANY

God who grants wisdom and foresight, enter our hearts that our prayers may reflect your will for us and hear us as we say, Lord in your mercy, **hear our prayer.**

Endow your church with the courage to call for justice, peace, and mercy and grant it humility so that it may always be ready to reform itself to more perfectly reflect your glory.
Lord in your mercy, **hear our prayer.**

Inspire the leaders of the nations to pursue wisdom and generosity of spirit, that they may work together to build a world where all peoples may flourish and where war is a relic of the past.
Lord in your mercy, **hear our prayer.**

Bestow upon those gathered here today the desire to continue Christ's mission and ministry to our neighbors and to serve them with love.
Lord in your mercy, **hear our prayer.**

Open our eyes and hearts wide enough to take on the cares and challenges that threaten our environment and empower us to be effective stewards of your Creation.
Lord in your mercy, **hear our prayer.**

Bring healing and a sense of wellness to all who suffer, lift their pain, and grant them peace. [Especially we ask on behalf of…*prayer list*.]
Lord in your mercy, **hear our prayer.**

Bid welcome to the dying, that they, and we, may be comforted in their passing, trusting in your covenant with us and in the redeeming power of Christ.
Lord in your mercy, **hear our prayer.**

We cannot know the future, but we can depend upon your promises which you have delivered through your prophets and especially through the life, death, and resurrection of Jesus, who with you and the Holy Spirit reigns above now and always. **Amen.**

FIFTH SUNDAY AFTER THE EPIPHANY

Set us free from division and distraction and make your church a home for generous love. Hear us as we pray, Lord in your mercy, hear our prayer.

Free our leaders, and those who hold power and authority over others, from everything but justice and compassion. Make us a nation that comes together to serve all.
Lord in your mercy, **hear our prayer.**

Set us free from all persecution and oppression. Hold those who are in danger, imprisoned, hopeless and grieving in the palm of your hand.
Lord in your mercy, **hear our prayer.**

Free us in all our towns and communities, cities and neighborhoods from comparison and competition and help us come together in ways that surprise and delight us.
Lord in your mercy, **hear our prayer.**

Set us free from disease and grief, pouring your healing love upon all those in any need of prayer. [We pray especially for...*prayer list.*]
Lord in your mercy, **hear our prayer.**

Free the dying from the bonds of this life in sure and certain knowledge that they are leaving this life to find new birth in you.
Lord in your mercy, **hear our prayer.**

We offer these prayers and praises Father in thanksgiving for the liberty and choice you give us in this life of faith and in hope of the life to come. In Jesus name. **Amen.**

SIXTH SUNDAY AFTER THE EPIPHANY

Healing God, soothe what troubles our hearts and souls and answer our prayers as we say, Lord in your mercy, hear our prayer.

Embolden your church to strengthen what is good and correct what is amiss; show us how to more fully embrace our call to be the body of Christ in the world.
Lord in your mercy, **hear our prayer.**

Answer our longings for peace throughout the world; show us how to be agents of peace and reconciliation.
Lord in your mercy, **hear our prayer.**

Grant to this congregation freedom from fears and grant to us discerning hearts for ministry; show us how to be good neighbors.
Lord in your mercy, **hear our prayer.**

Increase our wisdom that we might find answers for our climate challenge and courage to carry them out, show us how to tend your Creation.
Lord in your mercy, **hear our prayer.**

Bring healing to all who suffer, command your angels to watch over us, and increase our faith; show us how to face our fears with courage and grace. [Especially we lift up...*prayer list*.]
Lord in your mercy, **hear our prayer.**

Open the gates to your presence for all who have died that they may rest in your eternal care; show us your power over death.
Lord in your mercy, **hear our prayer.**

God of unknowable power, you have never failed to hold your people in your care and to offer to them the path to wholeness and peace. Continue to walk with us and guide us in the pathway of your Son, our Lord, Jesus Christ. **Amen.**

SEVENTH SUNDAY AFTER THE EPIPHANY

Most gracious and loving God, hear us as we pray: Lord in your mercy, hear our prayer.

Your greatest gift to us is love. Give your church such love for you that the world is transformed by the worship of you and service in your name.
Lord in your mercy, **hear our prayer.**

Give this nation and its leaders a love for all people so that all who live here may be strengthened and encouraged. And may we be heartened to know that, even now, you are calling new generations of people who long to serve your people.
Lord in your mercy, **hear our prayer.**

Send your peace into the world, that all people might have food, shelter, opportunity, freedom and a deep knowledge and love of you.
Lord in your mercy, **hear our prayer.**

Grant peace and prosperity to the people who live in this community, to the people we live and work with, to the people in these pews. Let the love of you fill our neighborhoods with a sense of togetherness and peace.
Lord in your mercy, **hear our prayer.**

Your love can heal all things and make all things new. Rain your healing power down upon those who are ill, or anxious, or in need. [We pray especially for these brothers and sisters, asking you to do what is best for each of them...*prayer list*.]
Lord in your mercy, **hear our prayer.**

You promised us that your love does not end when we die. Comfort those who mourn and bring the dying into the saving light of your kingdom.
Lord in your mercy, **hear our prayer.**

God of our hope, hear our earnest prayers and shine your grace upon us; through Jesus Christ our Lord who lives and reigns with you and the Holy Spirit. One God now and forever. **Amen.**

EIGHTH SUNDAY AFTER THE EPIPHANY

God of Spirit, God of glory we come to you now with our needs and our hopes that you might hear and respond as we say, **Lord in your mercy, hear our prayer.**

We pray that your church might always have its eyes on your promised future as it ministers to the needs of today.
Lord in your mercy, **hear our prayer.**

We pray that this nation and its leaders might look beyond its divisions and strive to build a place where the equal dignity and liberty of all its inhabitants might be recognized and celebrated.
Lord in your mercy, **hear our prayer.**

We pray that this assembly might feel your presence as it gathers and confident in its belovedness might work together and in joy to bring your love to our neighbors.
Lord in your mercy, **hear our prayer.**

We pray for the earth and all its creatures that this amazing oasis of abundant life might be preserved and healed from all the ways we have wounded it.
Lord in your mercy, **hear our prayer.**

We pray for the sick and the suffering, for the oppressed and the marginalized, that they might recover their wholeness and know the peace of your healing Spirit. [For...*prayer list.*]
Lord in your mercy, **hear our prayer.**

We pray for the dead and the dying that they might be welcomed into your eternal embrace, and we pray for the grieving that they too might find peace in your promises.
Lord in your mercy, **hear our prayer.**

Merciful and generous God, you have provided through your creation all that we might need, and we pray that through your Spirit the world might find all its longings answered and all its fears borne away so that we might live into the full goodness of what you have wrought. All this we ask through Christ, our Lord, who with you and the Holy Spirit are united as One God, indivisible and almighty. **Amen.**

LAST SUNDAY AFTER THE EPIPHANY

Lord, on this last Sunday before the beginning of Lent we ask that you bless this congregation with open hearts and a desire to prepare for You. May our words be acceptable in your sight as we pray, Lord in your mercy, hear our prayer.

When we believe that we know the only way to follow you Lord, give your church the blessing of humility.
Lord in your mercy, **hear our prayer.**

When we believe our nation is an island without obligations to our neighbors, when we feel no need to pray for those who differ from us. Give your people the blessing of shame.
Lord in your mercy, **hear our prayer.**

When we believe our community exists only for our needs and not to serve the greater good that supports even those who live very different lives from us, give us the blessing of neighborliness.
Lord in your mercy, **hear our prayer.**

When we turn a blind eye to violence and persecution due to our own desire for wealth or comfort, bless us with the ability to repent and turn to you.
Lord in your mercy, **hear our prayer.**

When we pray for the sick and suffering, bless them with the healing power of your love. [Especially we pray for...*prayer list.*]
Lord in your mercy, **hear our prayer.**

When we allow fear to rob us of the comfort that you bring to the dying, bless us with the conviction that you have prepared a place for each of us.
Lord in your mercy, **hear our prayer.**

Bless us Lord with hearts that love, with minds that turn to you often and hands that comfort, hold and pray. In the name of your Son, who resides with you and the Holy Spirit this day and always. **Amen.**

FIRST SUNDAY IN LENT

God of hope, we acknowledge and lament the ways in which we are deficient while holding close to your promises as offer to you the deepest needs and desires of our hearts, saying, Lord in your mercy, hear our prayer.

Shine brightly in your church that your glory may not be missed and that its calling may be clear.
Lord in your mercy, **hear our prayer.**

Dispel the fears and hatreds that fester in our nation and lead us astray from pursuing the common good.
Lord in your mercy, **hear our prayer.**

Lead this congregation through this Lenten season so that we may, with contrite hearts and willing spirits, reform and amend our ways, strengthen our faith, and acknowledge your authority in our lives.
Lord in your mercy, **hear our prayer.**

In the challenges we face grant us the courage and perseverance to answer and resolve them that your glorious creation might be healed, and human society reconciled to you.
Lord in your mercy, **hear our prayer.**

Mend what is broken, make whole what has been fractured, and relieve the suffering of all who are sick or oppressed in any way. [Especially we pray for...*prayer list.*]
Lord in your mercy, **hear our prayer.**

Draw close to you those who have died and give them rest, comfort those who mourn, and keep us on the path that leads to you and reunion with those whose whom we have lost.
Lord in your mercy, **hear our prayer.**

Lord God, keep us safe from the trials of temptation and evil, keep our eyes on your promises, and be with us always as we traverse the Way of Jesus, who is our Lord and Redeemer and who lives and reigns with you and the Holy Spirit, One God, forever and ever. **Amen.**

SECOND SUNDAY IN LENT

Let us pray that we might turn our hearts to all that keeps us mindful of the divine, offering our compassionate God our prayers by responding, Lord in your mercy, hear our prayer.

We give you thanks for the privilege of being your church. Help us keep this holy Lenten season faithfully and enthusiastically.
Lord in your mercy, **hear our prayer.**

We give you thanks for this nation and our leaders. Help them to stay the course of peace and service.
Lord in your mercy, **hear our prayer.**

We give you thanks for the many diverse and beautiful people you love on this planet we call home. Help us to care deeply for your people and your creation.
Lord in your mercy, **hear our prayer.**

We give you thanks for our homes and our families; for the lives and loves that we enjoy. Help our loved ones to believe that the church might be the place where they can find deep meaning in their lives again.
Lord in your mercy, **hear our prayer.**

We give you thanks for the way you care for each of us. Help our brothers and sisters to find healing of body, mind and spirit. [We pray especially for…*prayer list.*]
Lord in your mercy, **hear our prayer.**

We give you thanks for the abiding love you have for all those who labor to leave this life and come home to you. Help those who grieve to know that you are present in this and all things.
Lord in your mercy, **hear our prayer.**

All this we ask through your Son Jesus Christ, for whom we offer you thanks and praise, this day and always. **Amen.**

THIRD SUNDAY IN LENT

God of Strength, answer swiftly the needs of your people and hear our prayers as we say, Lord in your mercy, hear our prayer.

Nourish the faith of your church that it might vigorously take up the work of the gospel to share your love with the world.
Lord in your mercy **hear our prayer.**

Instill in our leaders a hunger for justice and peace that the policies they pursue might bring forth a world without war and rancor, where all people share in the bounty of creation.
Lord in your mercy **hear our prayer.**

Renew our faith and give us hearts burning to serve our neighbors that the love of the Christ might be made manifest.
Lord in your mercy **hear our prayer.**

Grant to us your creative spirit as we seek to build a sustainable and life-giving society in harmony with the natural world you have so lovingly crafted.
Lord in your mercy **hear our prayer.**

Shower your blessings on those who suffer or are in need, that they may know healing and peace. [We pray especially for those who have sought our prayer, for…*prayer list*.]
Lord in your mercy **hear our prayer.**

Welcome the dying into the chorus of praise which eternally surrounds you and grant us an entrance into your loving presence when we depart this world.
Lord in your mercy **hear our prayer.**

Loving God, you have showed us time and again the path to abundant life, keep us walking on the pathways of Christ that lead to heavenly joy. All this we ask in the name of the one who is our redeemer and savior, Jesus Christ. **Amen.**

FOURTH SUNDAY IN LENT

Open your hearts and offer to God the needs of people and the hopes of the world as we pray Lord in your mercy, hear our prayer.

As your church, Lord God, we give you thanks for the miracle of the loaves and fishes and for those miracles that occur in our lives today.
Lord in your mercy, **hear our prayer.**

As a nation of people who enjoy freedoms and opportunities that others do not have, we pray that you will look with favor upon those nations in greatest need and bring them to a place of safety and abundance.
Lord in your mercy, **hear our prayer.**

As stewards of your creation, we give thanks to you for the wonders you have given into our care. We pray for the protection of all animals everywhere, those who are our close companions, those who roam in hidden places or soar toward heaven or swim in the deep, that they will thrive and survive in this world that we often abuse.
Lord in your mercy, **hear our prayer.**

We pray that you will fill our hearts with a need to provide for those who have no home, no safety net, and no way forward. As physical beings subject to illness and accident, we ask for your healing upon those brothers and sisters who are suffering, that they might be restored to full health and purpose. [We pray for...*prayer list.*]
Lord in your mercy, **hear our prayer.**

As spiritual beings who put our trust in you, bring us at our last to that heavenly place where with all your saints we might find everlasting rest.
Lord in your mercy, **hear our prayer.**

Holy Trinity, Father, Son, and Spirit of God, hear these prayers we offer to you today, fulfilling them as may be best for us. **Amen.**

FIFTH SUNDAY IN LENT

God of Promise, listen now to our prayers and answer them as may be best for us as we say, Lord in your mercy, hear our prayer.

Lift up your people and lead us on the path of righteousness, that working together as one body across the globe we might bring the love of Christ to the whole world.
Lord in your mercy, **hear our prayer.**

Lead the nations into the ways of peace, let enemies be reconciled, and bonds of friendship strengthened for the well-being of all peoples.
Lord in your mercy, **hear our prayer.**

Be present to all gathered here today, be their strong foundation and the light that leads them into abundant life.
Lord in your mercy, **hear our prayer.**

Help us to be advocates and guardians of your created world, show us how to preserve and sustain the beauty and bounty of the natural world.
Lord in your mercy, **hear our prayer.**

Give strength in our weakness, courage in our fear, and hope in our despair. Bring healing to all who suffer and lift up those who are pressed down.
[Especially we pray for...*prayer list*.]
Lord in your mercy, **hear our prayer.**

Give comfort to those who are grieving, quiet the anxieties of the dying, and grant them entrance into the promise of your eternal presence.
Lord in your mercy, **hear our prayer.**

Lord, you have placed the love of your will in our hearts, show us how to better reflect that love into the world, that it may be transformed by your glory. With thanksgiving and hopefulness, we ask these things in the name of Christ, who with you and the Holy Spirit lives and reigns, one God, now and always. **Amen.**

LECTIONARY YEAR B

SUNDAY OF THE PASSION - PALM SUNDAY

In earnest reverence and faith, we offer up the needs and desires of our hearts as we say, Lord in your mercy, hear our prayer.

Christ came in modesty to shake and overturn the powers of the world, grant that your church may always walk humbly but also unafraid to stand for those most in need and against those who would oppress or abuse them.
Lord in your mercy, **hear our prayer.**

Shower wisdom and perseverance on those who lead and serve this nation, guide them into forbearance and patience in their dealings with other nations that this nation and all nations may know peace and prosperity.
Lord in your mercy, **hear our prayer.**

Grow the bonds of love within this assembly and give us courage to grow that love and to share it with our neighbors.
Lord in your mercy, **hear our prayer.**

Let not our appetites overwhelm the abundance of creation, endow our hearts with discernment and our spirits with fortitude that we might begin the work of reimagining human life that sustainably meets all our needs.
Lord in your mercy, **hear our prayer.**

Ease the pains and worries of all who suffer, give them peace, and make them whole. [Especially we pray for…*prayer list.*]
Lord in your mercy, **hear our prayer.**

Guide the dying through the fear of death and bring them into the brightness of your eternal glory.
Lord in your mercy, **hear our prayer.**

Though we have not earned or deserved it, your love has been steadfast from the beginning. Give us courage that we should never deny our Lord but live always within his care. Our prayers we lift in the name of Jesus, our redeemer and advocate, who lives and reigns with you and the Holy Spirit, forever and ever. **Amen.**

MAUNDY THURDAY

Hear us O God as you have promised and respond as may be best for us as we lift our voices in prayer saying, Lord in your mercy, hear our prayer.

May your church be a sacrament to the world, showing forth your love to the world, strengthened by the Holy Spirit, and led by the teachings and example of our Lord, Jesus Christ
Lord in your mercy, **hear our prayer.**

May our nation be blessed with leaders who serve with humility and the desire to work on behalf of all.
Lord in your mercy, **hear our prayer.**

May your creation be healed of the damage we have done and may we be advocates of new and better ways of living that are sustainable and life-giving.
Lord in your mercy, **hear our prayer.**

May your people gathered here be ever mindful of the love of Christ and inspired by his example to embrace his way and be your agents of love in a hurting world.
Lord in your mercy, **hear our prayer.**

May all who know sickness and pain know your healing presence in their lives and be made whole and at peace.
Lord in your mercy, **hear our prayer.**

May the dead be remade through your eternal love and rise again in your new age.
Lord in your mercy, **hear our prayer.**

Through Christ you have gifted us with all we need for the abundant life you have offered. Remember your love for us and lead us ever deeper into relationship with you and with one another, through Christ we pray, who with you and the Holy Spirit are One God, eternal and almighty. **Amen.**

EASTER *Early or Vigil Service*

Alleluia Christ is Risen! Hear our prayers offered this night from hearts gladdened by the hope of eternal life as we say, Lord in your mercy, hear our prayer.

Grant your church to always hold fast to the example of Christ's life and the hope of His resurrection.
Lord in your mercy, **hear our prayer.**

Fill the hearts of this nation with hope, peace, and a willingness to work together to build a nation where everyone has the opportunity to thrive and to live into their potential.
Lord in your mercy, **hear our prayer.**

Inhabit the lives of all gathered here; be light that dispels all darkness, vanquishing our fears and giving us the courage to love boldly.
Lord in your mercy, **hear our prayer.**

Fill our hearts with gratitude and thankfulness for the marvelous and abundant diversity of life and empower us to be stewards of your creation that all future generations may glory in all that you have created for us.
Lord in your mercy, **hear our prayer.**

Bring wholeness and healing to all who suffer in body, mind, or spirit, that they might have peace and abundant life.
Lord in your mercy, **hear our prayer.**

We give thanks for the lives of those who have already entered into your glory, and we ask that we too may one day arise in your eternal kingdom.
Lord in your mercy, **hear our prayer.**

Most gracious God, in Christ your love was made manifest in our world, embolden us to courageously continue his ministry and to face without fear where love might take us confident in Christ's promise to stand with us and walk with us always. **Amen.**

EASTER *Principal Service*

Gracious God whose love defeated even death, hear and answer our deepest hopes and needs as you did for the women who discovered the empty tomb and hear our prayers as we say, Lord in your mercy, **hear our prayer.**

Your church is the Body of Christ, constituted and empowered to continue to proclaim Christ's resurrection; strengthen and embolden us to be persistent in our proclamation.
Lord in your mercy, **hear our prayer.**

Our world still falls short of the full blossoming of human potential; open the eyes and hearts of the world's leaders to pursue peace and human thriving for all people.
Lord in your mercy, **hear our prayer.**

Help us to see the risen Christ in the world around; guide us into the work you have given us to do so that the ministries of Jesus might continue; that the world might know his healing and love through our actions.
Lord in your mercy, **hear our prayer.**

You have placed us in a glorious creation and charged us with its care; grant us wisdom and a willingness to protect our environment so that future generations might know the fullness of its beauty and abundance.
Lord in your mercy, **hear our prayer.**

Bring healing and wholeness to our lives and to all who suffer in any way; grant that they
might feel Christ's caring touch on their hurts. [Especially we pray for... *prayer list.*]
Lord in your mercy, **hear our prayer.**

Christ's resurrection opened for us the way to eternal life; grant that we all may continue on Christ's pathway and enter into your eternal reign and rise again with all the saints who have gone before.
Lord in your mercy, **hear our prayer.**

Glorious Lord, you have promised to be with us always fulfill now your promises for us and grant our prayers as may be best of us and always in accord with your will. All this we ask through our advocate and redeemer, Christ Jesus who lives with you and the Holy Spirit, eternally one God. **Amen.**

MONDAY IN EASTER WEEK

With gladness of hearts, we make haste to offer you our prayers, Risen Lord, saying, Lord in your mercy, hear our prayer.

Like our sister Mary of Magdala, we too long to see you, Christ. Open your disciples in this age to the reality of your presence among us and send us anew into the joyful task of shouting out good news.
Lord in your mercy, **hear our prayer.**

May our government and all its leaders embody your care for justice and mercy. May our leaders in towns and counties and cities and capitals rejoice in serving others and may the world stage see an end to the evil of war and a reorientation toward a global goal of peace.
Lord in your mercy, **hear our prayer.**

Open our eyes to see the needs in our own neighborhoods and parishes. Use us to answer prayers and to be a healing presence to those around us.
Lord in your mercy, **hear our prayer.**

Blanket this community with peace and concord. Give us an appreciation for our neighbors and a desire to know them well. Give us your love for the world around us.
Lord in your mercy, **hear our prayer.**

Bless and heal those who are anxious of heart, hopeless in spirit or ill. Give them relief from suffering and a sense of wholeness and peace.
Lord in your mercy, **hear our prayer.**

We pray for the departed with a special care for those who mourn their passing. Welcome them with light and joy into your kingdom.
Lord in your mercy, **hear our prayer.**

With joy in the promises given through Christ's resurrection, these prayers are offered in a spirit of love to you Eternal God, giving thanks to you, your Son, our savior, and the Holy Spirit. **Amen.**

TUESDAY IN EASTER WEEK

We lift up our voices in prayer and supplication, saying, Lord in your mercy, hear our prayer.

You have given to your people, the church, the gift of the Holy Spirit to lead us into greater love and greater understanding, grant us the strength to follow.
Lord in your mercy, **hear our prayer.**

Fill the hearts of this world's leaders with a desire to be servants to justice and mercy and to see the dignity of all people, grant us the peace which passes understanding.
Lord in your mercy, **hear our prayer.**

Inspire our imaginations to find ways to undo the damage we have done to the environment and climate, grant us the courage to make bold changes.
Lord in your mercy, **hear our prayer.**

Grow in us the joy we have experienced through Christ's resurrection and give us willing hearts and hands to continue His work in this community. Grant us resilience to continue our mission.
Lord in your mercy, **hear our prayer.**

Arouse in us the faith to see in Christ's victory an invitation to abundant life in the here and now. Grant us hearts overflowing with joyous love.
Lord in your mercy, **hear our prayer.**

Let your healing spirit descend upon all who suffer. Grant them release from their pain and fears.
Lord in your mercy, **hear our prayer.**

Welcome the dying, comfort the grieving, and bring us, at the end of our earthly journey into your loving embrace. Grant us all the fulfillment of your promises.
Lord in your mercy, **hear our prayer.**

Through Christ your power entered into the world in new and wondrous ways, enter into our lives that we may know and share your glorious love that transforms all human life. We ask this through the one who has conquered death and opened the pathway to eternal life for all people, this same Christ who with You and the Holy Spirit lives and reigns, forever. **Amen.**

WEDNESDAY IN EASTER WEEK

Risen and holy Savior, we know you in the breaking of bread and the sharing of the cup of your new covenant. As we wait in anticipation for that holy meal, we offer you the crumbs of our hearts as we say, Lord in your mercy, hear our prayer.

Grant your church a spirit that allows us to take on and tackle projects that will improve our ministry, serve our neighbors and better our own spiritual lives
Lord in your mercy: **hear our prayer.**

Grant our nation a spirit of renewal, revival, and respect for one another and for those who live in different countries and circumstances than we do.
Lord in your mercy: **hear our prayer.**

Give to people in every place those things that are necessary for life – food, shelter, clothing, friends, gratifying work, and meaningful worship of you.
Lord in your mercy: **hear our prayer.**

Grant that all those who feel isolated and alone may turn to a true follower of Jesus and find a place to worship, to grow and to be in community.
Lord in your mercy: **hear our prayer.**

Give to all those who lead or manage others in government, workplaces, homes, and churches the integrity to do what is right, joy in the work they are called to do, and wisdom to avoid temptation.
Lord in your mercy: **hear our prayer.**

Grant healing to those who are sick, suffering or in need.
Lord in your mercy: **hear our prayer.**

Give the dying a place at your heavenly banquet and grant them peace at their end.
Lord in your mercy: **hear our prayer.**

These prayers and praises are yours, Almighty Father, who together with your Son and the Holy Spirit, reign this day and always. **Amen.**

THURSDAY IN EASTER WEEK

God of peace, enter in and hear us as we lift up our hopes and needs to you as we say, Lord in your mercy, hear our prayer.

That your church may be a non-anxious presence in a world wracked by turmoil and conflict and place of peace and sanctuary for all we pray.
Lord in your mercy, **hear our prayer.**

That this nation may fulfill its promises, offer dignity to all its people, and be an advocate for justice, mercy, and peace in the world we pray.
Lord in your mercy, **hear our prayer.**

That our local community might be a place where children might grow up in peace and security with opportunities to grow into the people they were created to be we pray.
Lord in your mercy, **hear our prayer.**

That this assembly might grow in faith and work together to discern and carry out your mission for us we pray.
Lord in your mercy, **hear our prayer.**

That those impacted by sickness and injury might find relief in your healing love, be returned to wholeness, and know the peace which is beyond comprehension we pray.
Lord in your mercy, **hear our prayer.**

That the dead might be made complete in your love and that we may all rise again together in your new age we pray.
Lord in your mercy, **hear our prayer.**

In Christ you have overcome the darkness which shrouded human life and given us freedom and reason for hope. In thankfulness for your salvation, we offer these prayers through Christ, who with you and the Holy Spirit stand over all creation forever. **Amen.**

FRIDAY IN EASTER WEEK

Remembering that Jesus showed love for his friends by sharing food and fellowship, let us pray for the followers of Jesus, for ourselves, and for the world as we say, Lord in your mercy, hear our prayer.

May our hearts and minds be always on you O God. Bless us with silence to hear your voice and share our thoughts with you.
Lord in your mercy: **hear our prayer.**

May our country be a place where children can thrive in their homes, in their families, their schools, and communities. Bless each young life with safety, confidence, and love.
Lord in your mercy: **hear our prayer.**

May our homes be free from anger and division. Bless each of us with patience in our relationships and peace in our households.
Lord in your mercy: **hear our prayer.**

May our communities be places of welcome for those who are not of our faith, our race, our politics, or our preferences. Bless us with the knowing of strangers and angels.
Lord in your mercy: **hear our prayer.**

May our prayers for healing be heard for these friends and acquaintances, that your grace might provide them with restoration.
Lord in your mercy, **hear our prayer.**

May our loved ones depart this life in confidence, without fear. Bless our own leaving with peace and the nearness of loved ones.
Lord in your mercy: **hear our prayer.**

When we are anxious and stray from you, O God. Keep us safely in your hands and hear our prayers for the world and its people. Grant them as may be best for us. In the name of the Father, the Son, and the Holy Spirit. **Amen.**

SATURDAY IN EASTER WEEK

We have gathered to offer you praise and ask for a response to our hopes and needs; hear us now as we pray; Lord in your mercy, hear our prayer.

Let your church be a herald of your Good News and a visible sign of your gracious love to all the world.
Lord in your mercy, **hear our prayer.**

Let our nation be a place of peace and goodwill amongst all people and a positive source of hope for all the world to see.
Lord in your mercy, **hear our prayer.**

Let us learn to be advocates for a peaceful and sustainable future that future generations may know the abundance of creation and call us blessed for our willingness to change.
Lord in your mercy, **hear our prayer.**

Let this assembly know of your presence with us and strengthen us to carry on your work of healing and reconciliation.
Lord in your mercy, **hear our prayer.**

Let all who suffer in any way know release from their pain, their worry, and their fear. Grant them wholeness and hope.
Lord in your mercy, **hear our prayer.**

Let the dying know of your love and of the welcome they will receive into your holy presence and let all of us see in death the hope won for us through the mighty passion of Christ.
Lord in your mercy, **hear our prayer.**

You have led your people through fear into promise again and again. Through Christ's resurrection give us courage to strive for the promise in our lives. All this we ask through the one who loves us and asks of us our whole selves, Jesus Christ, who with you and the Holy Spirit bestrides creation in this and all ages. **Amen.**

SECOND SUNDAY OF EASTER

Let us pray for ourselves and others, responding to each petition with "Lord in your mercy, hear our prayer.

Holy God, give your faithful people voices to proclaim the beautiful truth, that your son is risen!
Lord in your mercy, **hear our prayer.**

Holy One who rose again, give us hearts to serve your poor, to proclaim good news, to see you in all those we see this day and every day.
Lord in your mercy, **hear our prayer.**

Holy Spirit who proceeds from the father and the son, give this nation and its leaders a strong resolve to serve in love.
Lord in your mercy, **hear our prayer.**

Holy and just Lord of all, seek out the persecuted and give protection. Hear the cries of the imprisoned and give them peace. See the needs of your people and help us to respond with your help.
Lord in your mercy, **hear our prayer.**

Holy hope of the poor and suffering, grant healing to all those who experience pain and loss, sickness and depression, estrangement, and violence. [May these brothers and sisters know recovery of body mind and spirit this day…*prayer list.*]
Lord in your mercy, **hear our prayer.**

Holy comfort of the dying and strength for those who mourn, let light perpetual shine upon those who come to you, and love be their shelter in your heavenly kingdom.
Lord in your mercy, **hear our prayer.**

We offer these prayers and petitions in the name of Holy Love – Father, Son and Holy Spirit. **Amen.**

THIRD SUNDAY OF EASTER

Father of all creation, in glory and wonder we lift our voices, beseeching you to hear and respond as we say, Lord in your mercy, hear our prayer.

Infuse in your church urgency for the mission of love and reconciliation, that the world's divisions may be healed.
Lord in your mercy, **hear our prayer.**

Spread your wisdom to leaders of the nations, open their eyes to the power of grace and mercy for the thriving of their people.
Lord in your mercy, **hear our prayer.**

Grant to this congregation the peace of Christ, that we may, with courage and boldness, be the heart, hands, and lips of Jesus to our neighbors.
Lord in your mercy, **hear our prayer.**

Restore the full glory of nature and cure us of the impulses that lead to its degradation and destruction, so that we and all future generations may live sustainably in your Creation.
Lord in your mercy, **hear our prayer.**

Let your healing power be present in the lives of all who suffer in body, mind, or spirit. [Especially we lift up...*prayer list.*]
Lord in your mercy, **hear our prayer.**

Keep those who have died in your loving embrace and bring us at the end of our lives, into that place of glory and joy where we may be reunited with those who have gone before.
Lord in your mercy, **hear our prayer.**

Glorious God, you have shown us the power of your love in the resurrection of Jesus, hold us fast within that love, keep us forever in your glory and be ever present to us. We lift these prayers in the confidence of the promises of Jesus, our Lord and Savior. **Amen.**

FOURTH SUNDAY OF EASTER

Let us pray for the needs of the world, responding to each petition with Lord in your mercy, hear our prayer.

Lord you are the good shepherd, give your sheep ears that hear your voice and hearts that long to follow you.
Lord in your mercy, **hear our prayer.**

Shepherd of the church, deepen our faith and inspire us to turn to your holy word for daily reflection and comfort.
Lord in your mercy, **hear our prayer.**

Shepherd of those who love justice and truth, bless this nation with servant leaders and with those who long to better the lives of your people.
Lord in your mercy, **hear our prayer.**

Shepherd to those who love to learn, give our children a hunger to excel and imaginations that thirst for knowledge. Bless those who teach, coach, serve, protect, and nourish children in all nations.
Lord in your mercy, **hear our prayer.**

Shepherd of the sick and suffering, bless our friends and neighbors with healthy bodies, minds, and spirits. Take away the anxieties and afflictions of those with mental illness. Take away the apathy and hopelessness of spiritual sickness and heal those with physical illnesses. [Especially we pray for…*prayer list*.]
Lord in your mercy, **hear our prayer.**

Shepherd of souls, bless the dying with a peaceful end and comfort those who wait and watch for their passing; that both are in full awareness that you are near.
Lord in your mercy, **hear our prayer.**

Hear us, O holy and most gracious protector, shepherd our lives from our beginning to our ending, who with your son and holy spirit reign forever and ever. **Amen.**

FIFTH SUNDAY OF EASTER

God of life, we have gathered within the shelter of your promises, hear now our longings and hopes, that you might be present and answer them as may be best for us as we say, Lord in your mercy, hear our prayer.

Tend to your church, that it might bear the good fruits of faith, hope, and love for the welfare of the whole world.
Lord in your mercy, **hear our prayer.**

Let the leaders of the nations perceive the power of justice, peace, and liberty to bring about human flourishing.
Lord in your mercy, **hear our prayer.**

Aid us in nurturing faith in our lives, that your love may grow in us, transforming our lives and the lives of those we encounter each day.
Lord in your mercy, **hear our prayer.**

Encourage in us the desire to be effective stewards of the created world; let us with courage and hope respond to the environmental challenges we face.
Lord in your mercy, **hear our prayer.**

Shower grace on all who suffer, surround them with your love that they may find peace and healing from their trials. [We pray especially for… *prayer list.*]
Lord in your mercy, **hear our prayer.**

We pray that all who have died may rise again in your eternal presence and let the faithfulness of their lives inform and inspire our own.
Lord in your mercy, **hear our prayer.**

The world has been transformed through the faithful action of generations past, show us how we might abide in your Word and answer the needs of today with perseverance and courage. All we ask we ask through Christ our Lord, who with the you and the Holy Spirit stand above and sustain all creation across time and beyond. **Amen.**

SIXTH SUNDAY OF EASTER

Let us pray for God's people and the world saying, Lord in your mercy, hear our prayer.

Holy One we are your church, help those who long to know you find you here. Help us to leave this place and share your love.
Lord in your mercy, **hear our prayer.**

You tell us to abide in you; help us to make this nation a place where all can worship you in freedom and peace, respecting the dignity and rights of others.
Lord in your mercy, **hear our prayer.**

You ask us to love one another; show us how to serve our hungry, homeless, and threatened neighbors in your name.
Lord in your mercy, **hear our prayer.**

You call us to new ways of leadership; make our community, state, national, and global leaders servants of your justice and peace.
Lord in your mercy, **hear our prayer.**

You shelter those who are in harm's way and ask us to speak for the needs and rights of others. Give us courage to speak.
Lord in your mercy, **hear our prayer.**

You heal us with forgiveness and mercy. Shelter the sick with the peace and surety of your healing grace. [We pray especially for…*prayer list.*]
Lord in your mercy, **hear our prayer.**

You have loved us over generations. We give you thanks for those who have gone before us, and for those who are mourning now.
Lord in your mercy, **hear our prayer.**

You are our God, and we give you thanks, asking your blessing on these, our petitions as may be best for us, in full confidence of your love for us, In Jesus' name, **Amen.**

SEVENTH SUNDAY OF EASTER

Sovereign God, we beseech you to hear and respond to our prayers as we say, Lord in your mercy, hear our prayer.

Guide and encourage your church that Christ may be gloried through its actions and your love known in its proclamations and prayers.
Lord in your mercy, **hear our prayer.**

Dwell in the hearts of all who hold authority in our lives, that they might lead us with mercy and justice and work to build a society where all are given the opportunity to live into their created potential.
Lord in your mercy, **hear our prayer.**

Let the love of God be present in this assembly and in all we do as your people in this place.
Lord in your mercy, **hear our prayer.**

In the command to love God is the expectation of loving God's creation, let us love it with an eye towards ensuring its abundance is shared equitably and its bounty secured for all future generations.
Lord in your mercy, **hear our prayer.**

Mend whatever is broken in the lives of those who suffer, bring them peace and a sense of wholeness through your healing love. [Especially we pray for…*prayer list.*]
Lord in your mercy, **hear our prayer.**

Welcome the dying into your embrace, grant them entry into the company of saints, and reunite us with them at the end of our own earthly journey.
Lord in your mercy, **hear our prayer.**

Answer our hopes and desires that our joy may be made complete through your love and mercy and aid is becoming more fully the people you created us to be. Through Christ our Lord we ask these things in the confidence of your promises. **Amen.**

PENTECOST

May your Spirit stir up in us a powerful sense of hope as we lift our prayers to you saying, Lord in your mercy, hear our prayer.

The Spirit has come to lead your people into deeper understanding and deeper relationship with you, give your church the courage to go where it leads us.
Lord in your mercy, **hear our prayer.**

Inspire this nation, that we might pursue your ways of justice, mercy, and dignity so that the people of this land might live together in peace and unity, working together towards a more perfect union.
Lord in your mercy, **hear our prayer.**

May the Spirit of God be a cleansing wind in our lives, that we might embody the righteousness of Christ in our lives, through faith, and take up his work on behalf of our neighbors.
Lord in your mercy, **hear our prayer.**

Rouse us out of complacency and apathy, and galvanize our commitment to creating a sustainable future for all people that the abundance of creation might be available to all future generations.
Lord in your mercy, **hear our prayer.**

Enter into the lives of all who know pain, fear, illness, and anxiety that they might know the freedom of your healing grace and live in the fullness of their belovedness. [Especially we pray for…prayer list.]
Lord in your mercy, **hear our prayer.**

Welcome into the fellowship of the saints, all who die, that they may be made complete in the forge of your saving grace.
Lord in your mercy, **hear our prayer.**

God of Wisdom and Knowledge, you have always sought to bring us into the full goodness of your creation, may we ever perceive and follow your Holy Spirit that our lives might reflect your glory and love. All this we ask in the name of Christ who with the Holy Spirit and You are One God over heaven and earth for all time. **Amen.**

TRINITY SUNDAY

Let us give glory to the One God in Three Persons and offer our needs and thanksgivings saying, Lord in your mercy, hear our prayer.

For the whole church of God, that we might find unity in mission and work towards reconciliation that your people might be one just as our God is One.
Lord in your mercy, **hear our prayer.**

For the nation and its leaders at every level, fill them with desire and encourage them to seek real solutions to our problems, and to seek always the common good.
Lord in your mercy, **hear our prayer.**

For the creation, that we might be effective stewards and use the abundant resources you have given us wisely and sustainably.
Lord in your mercy, **hear our prayer.**

For this parish and its people, that we might discern your will for us and deploy the gifts you have given us to build the kingdom of God through our daily lives.
Lord in your mercy, **hear our prayer.**

For all who suffer in any way, that your healing presence might be known in their lives. [Especially we pray for...*prayer list*].
Lord in your mercy, **hear our prayer.**

For those who have died and for those who grieve, that may know comfort in your embrace, and that we all might rise again in your new age.
Lord in your mercy, **hear our prayer.**

God of mystery, God of love, surround us and fill us with your grace, embolden us to be your agents of love in a hurting world, and answer our prayers as may be best for us and always to your glory. All this we ask through Christ, our Lord. **Amen.**

LECTIONARY YEAR B

PROPER 1: *Sunday closest to May 11*

Hear our prayers that we, and the world, may be made holy and brought into your vision of the kingdom that will come when we say, Lord in your mercy, hear our prayer.

When your people gather to worship you, bring about a conversion of heart that they may leave filled with your Holy Spirit.
Lord in your mercy, **hear our prayer.**

When this nation prays for our strength and prosperity, bless the poor and uncertain with strong advocates in all levels of our government and make us a country where all can thrive.
Lord in your mercy, **hear our prayer.**

When we think about our greatest hopes for those we love, let us be strong advocates for these same goals to be attainable for those of every neighborhood, race, and circumstance.
Lord in your mercy, **hear our prayer.**

When we gather with our families and friends, keep us open to the need to invite others into the blessing of relationships. Keep us mindful of those who are isolated and alone.
Lord in your mercy, **hear our prayer.**

When we struggle with depression, disillusionment, despair, and destructive behaviors, keep us ready to admit our failures and renew our determination to continue to turn away from sin and toward your love.
Lord in your mercy, **hear our prayer.**

When we are sick or suffering, bless our healing lord. [We pray especially for...*prayer list*].
Lord in your mercy, **hear our prayer.**

When we are close to death and near the end of this life, give us faith in your promises that we will not be left alone or apart from you. Bless the grieving with the promise of your Son.
Lord in your mercy, **hear our prayer.**

When we are sure that we do not know how to pray, bless us with your willingness to listen to our hearts; through Jesus Christ our Lord, who lives and reigns with you and the Holy Spirit, one God, now and forever. **Amen.**

PROPER 2: *Sunday closest to May 18*

God our teacher, you show us the paths our hearts and souls should follow, hear now our longings and hopes as we say, Lord in your mercy, hear our prayer.

Keep your church focused on continuing the ministries of Jesus with clarity and determination for the sake of a world that is in need of your transforming grace.
Lord in your mercy, **hear our prayer.**

Abide in the deliberations of our leaders and the leaders of all nations. Let them seek peace, reconciliation, and the welfare of all peoples.
Lord in your mercy, **hear our prayer.**

Be present in the worship and ministry of this assembly. Keep us focused on our call to be the body of Christ and on continuing the work of Christ in our community.
Lord in your mercy, **hear our prayer.**

Embolden us to face our climate challenges with courage, hope, and commitment; for with your aid, we know that they can be overcome.
Lord in your mercy, **hear our prayer.**

Give us grace to be present for those who suffer and grant them relief from their pain and lead them into peace and wellness. [We pray especially for… *prayer list.*]
Lord in your mercy, **hear our prayer.**

Gather the dead into your eternal loving arms, that your purpose for them may be fulfilled.
Lord in your mercy, **hear our prayer.**

O God of power and might, you have promised wholeness to your people and shown us how we might stand and take up the abundant life as shown to us by Jesus Christ, who with you and the Holy Spirit we worship and revere. **Amen.**

PROPER 3: *Sunday closest to May 25*

Let us bless the Lord and offer to God prayers for the beloved and the work of our hands, saying, Lord in your mercy, hear our prayer.

Lord, bless your church with wisdom and vulnerability that we might share the good news of the gospel with our very lives.
Lord in your mercy, **hear our prayer.**

Bless this nation with abundant food and life-giving purpose for all people. Give our leaders the right ideas and policies to protect and improve the way of life for all of us. Bless our civic leaders with support and encouragement for their efforts and advocacy.
Lord in your mercy, **hear our prayer.**

Lord, bless the world with peace and a shared sense that we are all members of the same family. Bring your salvation and comfort to all those with ears that long to hear your good news.
Lord in your mercy, **hear our prayer.**

Bless our homes with peace. Give us energy and strength to face what we must face, and the courage to embrace a life of faith in a world that offers different priorities than those of your Son. Give us lives that convey that a meaningful life is a beautiful life indeed.
Lord in your mercy, **hear our prayer.**

Bless the sick with cure and healing, and comfort those dealing with diagnosis and treatment with peace and confidence. [We pray especially for *…prayer list.*]
Lord in your mercy, **hear our prayer.**

Lord, bless the dying with comfort and love, the grieving with strength and community. We remember our loved ones, those who we held as role models and mentors, and we ask your continued blessing upon them and all those who enter your heavenly realm.
Lord in your mercy, **hear our prayer.**

We ask these prayers in the hope of your coming and in gratitude for the possibilities for new life that are ours even now. Through the grace of your son and the Holy Spirit who live and reign with you in your heavenly kingdom. **Amen.**

PROPER 4: *Sunday closest to June 1*

Good and giving God, who provides for us all good things, incline your ear to hear our prayers and respond to us as we say, Lord in your mercy, hear our prayer.

Keep your church holy, focus its efforts on furthering your mission of salvation, and let it be herald of good news to all people.
Lord in your mercy, **hear our prayer.**

Keep our nation and its leaders under your watchful eye, that we might work towards a more perfect union, and build a nation of promise and hope for all its inhabitants.
Lord in your mercy, **hear our prayer.**

Keep this assembly mindful of its call to be the body Christ in this neighborhood, that we and our neighbors might experience your love.
Lord in your mercy, **hear our prayer.**

Keep us mindful of the ways we can contribute to and further the healing of our natural world, that its full abundance might be restored and sustained.
Lord in your mercy, **hear our prayer.**

Keep all who suffer within your healing embrace; let them know wholeness, peace, and a secure knowledge in your presence in their lives.
Lord in your mercy, **hear our prayer.**

Keep us all in your grace and protection until we draw our last breaths and then welcome us into the glory of your eternal presence.
Lord in your mercy, **hear our prayer.**

You have cared for us and maintained us through the generations through your abundant mercy and grace; hold us close, now and tomorrow, that we might live more fully into your command to love with our whole selves that your transforming glory might dispel all the darkness which haunts our world. We ask all this through our Lord and Savior, Jesus Christ, who lives and reigns with you and the Holy Spirit, now and always. **Amen.**

PROPER 5: *Sunday closest to June 8*

In confidence we offer our prayers to the Lord, saying, Lord, in your mercy, hear our prayer.

That the church may always fix its gaze on the life that lasts forever, let us pray to the Lord.
Lord in your mercy, **hear our prayer.**

That all of humanity may be rescued from ignorance, disobedience, and death, let us pray to the Lord.
Lord in your mercy, **hear our prayer.**

That those who strive to build God's kingdom may enjoy the understanding and support of their families, let us pray to the Lord.
Lord in your mercy, **hear our prayer.**

That we may be filled with the power to amend our lives and to seek forgiveness from those we wrong, let us pray to the Lord.
Lord in your mercy, **hear our prayer.**

That our church may remain bound together in fidelity and compassion.
Lord in your mercy, **hear our prayer.**

That all those who are gathered here today may find trustworthy brothers and sisters in Christ, let us pray to the Lord.
Lord in your mercy, **hear our prayer.**

That all the sick and suffering may be healed, [Especially for...*prayer list*] let us pray to the Lord.
Lord in your mercy, **hear our prayer.**

In the communion of the Holy Spirit, and with all the saints who have entered into joy, let us commend our lives and the lives of one another to the Lord.
Lord in your mercy, **hear our prayer.**

God of loving-kindness, you have ordered all things for our benefit. Listen to our prayers and answer them with blessings. This we ask through Christ our Lord. **Amen.**

PROPER 6: *Sunday closest to June 15*

Creating, Redeeming, and Sustaining God, hear our prayers, for we offer them in faith and trust saying, Lord in your mercy, hear our prayer.

Hear us as we pray for the church, the place we feel your presence in Word and sacrament, and as we leave this good place, send us to the world to share your love.
Lord in your mercy, **hear our prayer.**

Hear us as we pray for this county, this state, this country which we love. Protect our freedoms and the freedoms of others. Give us leaders who embrace the complexity of our issues and who can see a way forward when we cannot discern a compromise. Give us an abundance to share with other nations and a peace that is never ending.
Lord in your mercy, **hear our prayer.**

Protect those who serve our nation, our state, our communities. Keep all those in uniform, in the military, in the medical field, in the fire and rescue departments, in police departments shielded from harm. As sad as it is, Lord, we also ask for the protection of your children, teachers, and people everywhere from the violence that comes from guns, poverty, mental illness, hopelessness and our own apathy and self-centeredness.
Lord in your mercy, **hear our prayer.**

Lord, we call on your miraculous love to heal those on our hearts today. Give them healing of body, healing of mind and an elevation and restoration of spirit. [Most especially...*prayer list.*]
Lord in your mercy, **hear our prayer.**

Bless the dying. Be in the hands of those who will care for them until the end, in the hearts of those who will mourn and bless them as they depart this world with your abundant light.
Lord in your mercy, **hear our prayer.**

May these prayers be only the first of many times this week we will remember to offer you our deepest longings for ourselves and others. Bless these prayers to our use and us to your service. In Jesus' Name. **Amen.**

PROPER 7: *Sunday closest to June 22*

Holy One, creator and sustainer of life, we come together in prayer to put before our needs and our hopes, that we may also know your peace.

We ask your presence as we seek to be your people, bless this church and all who minister in the name of Christ.
Lord in your mercy, **hear our prayer.**

We ask your wisdom to be upon our leaders as well as the leaders of the world, that working together, ours might be a world of peace, justice, and mercy.
Lord in your mercy, **hear our prayer.**

We ask for your guidance as we discern how to be faithful stewards of your creation, that we might equitably balance our needs with the needs of the whole world and the needs of future generations.
Lord in your mercy, **hear our prayer.**

We ask for your blessings for our homes and communities, that these might be places of hope, love, and charity.
Lord in your mercy, **hear our prayer.**

We ask for your healing presence in the lives of all who suffer distress in body, mind, or spirit. [Especially we ask on behalf of…*prayer list*.]
Lord in your mercy, **hear our prayer.**

We ask for your continuing mercy and salvation for those who have died and ask that we also may come to share in your kingdom.
Lord in your mercy, **hear our prayer.**

O God, let your peace which passes understanding be known to us, and answer our fears and hopes expressed in these prayers as may be best for us; and all this we ask through Christ, our Lord, who reigns with you and the Holy Spirit, One God now and always. **Amen.**

PROPER 8: *Sunday closest to June 29*

Gathered together with confidence in God's promise to be present with us, let us offer our hopes and needs in prayer saying, Lord in your mercy, hear our prayer.

We ask blessings of grace and perseverance to your church, that Christ's mission might continue, and His presence be known through us.
Lord in your mercy, **hear our prayer.**

We ask blessings of wisdom and compassion for our civic leaders, that our local community, our state, and our nation might be places of peace and human thriving.
Lord in your mercy, **hear our prayer.**

We ask blessings of discernment and generosity on our efforts to be effective stewards of your bountiful creation.
Lord in your mercy, **hear our prayer.**

We ask your healing power to bless the lives of all who suffer, especially we ask on behalf of those who have sought our prayer. [For…*prayer list.*]
Lord in your mercy, **hear our prayer.**

We ask blessings of peace and redemption on those who have died, and we ask that we might join with them again in your coming kingdom.
Lord in your mercy, **hear our prayer.**

Lord God, source of life and provider of all our needs; hear the prayers of your people, be present in our lives and answer our prayers as may be best for us and always to your glory. All this we ask through our Lord, your son, Jesus Christ. **Amen.**

LECTIONARY YEAR B

PROPER 9: *Sunday closest to July 6*

Holy God, you have promised to be in our midst when we gather in Christ's name; be with us now, hear our prayers, and respond to us in love and mercy, but always to your glory and in accord with your will. Let us offer our prayer saying, Lord in your mercy, hear our prayer.

Uphold and strengthen your church; open our eyes and ears to the prophets among us.
Lord in your mercy, **hear our prayer.**

Shine your light of wisdom upon this nation; lift up and strengthen what is good, root out what is evil. Open our eyes to its promise and give us strength to tear down what holds us back from being a nation of liberty, justice, and opportunity for all its people.
Lord in your mercy, **hear our prayer.**

Guide us in making wise choices for the care and sustainability of our environment, so that its abundance may be preserved for future generations.
Lord in your mercy, **hear our prayer.**

Embolden us to stand up for justice and mercy throughout our lives, so that our leaders might confidently craft righteous policies for the good of all people.
Lord in your mercy, **hear our prayer.**

Unleash the Holy Spirit in this congregation that we might boldly proclaim the Good News of Christ.
Lord in your mercy, **hear our prayer.**

Grant wholeness and freedom from fear or pain to all those who suffer from any affliction. [Especially we lift up...*prayer list.*]
Lord in your mercy, **hear our prayer.**

We know those who have died rest in your eternal care; grant that we, with them, may someday rise in your new age where heaven and earth are one.
Lord in your mercy, **hear our prayer.**

Merciful God, you know our needs before we ask, help us to see more clearly your call in our asking and make us shining lights of hope in the darkness. **Amen.**

PROPER 10: *Sunday closest to July 13*

Blessed God, we look for your response as we humbly lift up to you the hopes and longings of our hearts, saying, Lord in your mercy, hear our prayer.

Raise up leaders in your church whose hearts are true, that they may lead your people into greater love and unity.
Lord in your mercy, **hear our prayer.**

Strengthen the bonds of affection and mutual respect in our nation and among the leaders of the nations that peace and justice might be made manifest for all people.
Lord in your mercy, **hear our prayer.**

Build up the faith of this assembly, grant us wisdom and creativity to find new ways to answer your call of mission and ministry to our neighbors.
Lord in your mercy, **hear our prayer.**

Give us courage and strength to hold onto our hopes for better tomorrows. Show us how to be part of the sustainable solutions to the problems and challenges of our world.
Lord in your mercy, **hear our prayer.**

Be present to all who suffer, let them know peace and sense of wholeness and never let them feel alone in their struggle. [Especially we pray for… *prayer list.*]
Lord in your mercy, **hear our prayer.**

Grant to all who have died an entry into the eternal glory and joy of your presence.
Lord in your mercy, **hear our prayer.**

O God you have raised up your people and erected your church so that the promise of Christ and the ministry of Christ might continue and grow. Build us up that we too may respond to your invitation to love you and our neighbor. All this we ask through Christ our Lord, who with you and the Holy Spirit are one God, eternal and indivisible. **Amen.**

PROPER 11: *Sunday closest to July 20*

Loving God, you sustain and nurture us, offering wholeness and healing to our broken world and our sin-sick souls; we offer you our prayers in sure knowledge of your loving mercy towards us as we say, Lord in your mercy, hear our prayer.

You have chosen the Church as the vehicle of your mercy and compassion on earth, fill it with life, fill it with courage, fill it with zeal to fulfill your mission.
Lord in your mercy, **hear our prayer.**

Inspire the leaders of our nation to be generous of spirit that they might pursue policies that allow all people to thrive and flourish. Let all nations be reconciled, that we might live free of fear for one another and know true peace.
Lord in your mercy, **hear our prayer.**

Bless the places we call home, that they might be communities where everyone is able and encouraged to be who you created them to be; that together, we can build a world worthy of you.
Lord in your mercy, **hear our prayer.**

Bring your healing power to our lives and to those who suffer in body, mind, and spirit, especially for those who have sought the prayers of this congregation. [For…*prayer list.*]
Lord in your mercy, **hear our prayer.**

We stand between those generations who have shared your story but who no longer are with us on earth and those generations yet to come to whom we must share your story, embolden us as we await your return and sustain us and them until we all join you in the age to come.
Lord in your mercy, **hear our prayer.**

Lord, even in the deserted places you sustained your disciples and healed all who came to you. Sustain us also, answering our prayers as may be best for us and empowering us to continue your gospel mission. **Amen.**

PROPER 12: *Sunday closest to July 27*

Almighty God, in Christ you have shown us that your way is the way of compassion and mercy. We offer our prayers, in sure knowledge of your love, saying, Lord in your mercy, hear our prayer.

Lord, you fed multitudes and brought healing through your presence; empower and embolden your Church that we too might show forth compassion and mercy to a hurting world.
Lord in your mercy, **hear our prayer.**

Lord, bring wisdom to the leaders of our nation and of all the nations that they might seek peace and the flourishing of all people.
Lord in your mercy, **hear our prayer.**

Lord, our world is hungry - hungry for peace, for justice, for equality, and for a sustainable way of life. Inspire and sustain our commitment to build a world worthy of your sacrifice.
Lord in your mercy, **hear our prayer.**

Lord, help us to fulfill our potential in answering your call to be your people; to be your hands and feet in service to our community, that it might know and experience the abundance of your blessing.
Lord in your mercy, **hear our prayer.**

Lord, be present in the lives of those who suffer and strengthen those who care for them. Remind us, and urge us to offer love, compassion, and companionship to all in need. [Especially we ask your healing mercies for… *prayer list.*]
Lord in your mercy, hear our prayer.

Lord, guard those who have died, and tend those who grieve until the day when all will gather in your kingdom.
Lord in your mercy, hear our prayer.

Creating, redeeming, and sustaining God, you know the longings of our hearts and the desires of our souls; hear our prayers and fulfill them as may be best for us that we might know your saving grace and be filled with your never-ending love. **Amen.**

LECTIONARY YEAR B

PROPER 13: *Sunday closest to August 3*

O God, who fulfills us and invites us into ever deeper understanding and relationship, hear the prayers of your people as we offer ourselves, body and soul, to you saying, Lord in your mercy, hear our prayer

Protect and nurture your church, that it might share the feast of redemption with all who long for peace and connection to your life-giving Spirit.
Lord in your mercy, **hear our prayer.**

Instill wisdom and a yearning for peace in the hearts of the leaders of all nations, and grant to all in authority a zeal for compassion, mercy, and justice.
Lord in your mercy, **hear our prayer.**

Help us to see the abundance all around us and expel from our hearts and minds those fears that encumber our generosity.
Lord in your mercy, **hear our prayer.**

Embolden us to be the hands and feet of Christ in our local communities, that we might feed the hunger for food, for justice, for mercy and for dignity in a broken world.
Lord in your mercy, **hear our prayer.**

Remind us not to forget the lonely, the sick, the dying and all who suffer in body, mind, or spirit and spread your healing power in a hurting world. [Especially we hold up…*prayer list.*]
Lord in your mercy, **hear our prayer.**

The souls of the dead are in your care; strengthen those who grieve and grant that we may all one day walk together again in your new kingdom.
Lord in your mercy, **hear our prayer.**

Your promises are steadfast and sure O God, grant our desires as may be best for us and empower us to be your people. In thanksgiving to you, your son, and your Holy Spirit. **Amen.**

PROPER 14: *Sunday closest to August 10*

Who can separate us from the love of God? Let our hearts now respond to such overwhelming love as we pray together in the Spirit, saying, Lord in your mercy, hear our prayer.

That God will renew the merciful covenant made with us in love we pray.
Lord in your mercy, **hear our prayer.**

That the ministers of the gospel may be people of genuine conversion and prophetic voice, we pray.
Lord in your mercy, **hear our prayer.**

That the bread of life may be shared one day by all Christians at a common table of praise, we pray.
Lord, in your mercy, **hear our prayer.**

For the poor of our world, and for governments called to assist them in their need, we pray.
Lord in your mercy, **hear our prayer.**

For the sick and the suffering in our world. [Especially for...*prayer list.*]
Lord in your mercy, **hear our prayer.**

Let us be mindful of the dead. That they may come into the fullness of life, united with God in the communion of the faithful, we pray. Lord in your mercy, **hear our prayer.**

O God, your loving care for us calls for our gratitude. Multiply once again your abundant mercy toward us; renew your covenant with us; and let our hearts overflow with godly love for others. We ask this the name of Jesus, our Rabbi and Lord, now and in the Spirit and forever. **Amen.**

PROPER 15: *Sunday closest to August 17*

In confidence and longing we offer our needs and hopes to God in prayer as we say, Lord in your mercy, hear our prayer.

That your church may be a sacrament, a sure and certain sign of God's saving action in the world, we pray.
Lord in your mercy, **hear our prayer.**

That our nation might be a place of opportunity for all its people and a place where people may live with dignity and in concord with their neighbors, we pray.
Lord in your mercy, **hear our prayer.**

That this assembly might be a place where we encounter the living Christ and where we feel safe to be our truest created selves, we pray.
Lord in your mercy, **hear our prayer.**

That all the people of the world might come together to address our shared global problems and learn to live in peace, we pray.
Lord in your mercy, **hear our prayer.**

That those afflicted with illness or injury, those impacted by fear and oppression, and those who despair or are isolated might know relief from their distress and a sense of wholeness and connection, we pray. [Especially we pray for…*prayer list.*]
Lord in your mercy, **hear our prayer.**

That the dying may know peace in your eternal presence and that the grieving may know peace, we pray.
Lord in your mercy, **hear our prayer.**

Most Holy God, you have fed your people with your love and with the saving atonement of Christ. Walk with us that we might confidently travel the narrow path following in the footsteps of our Lord, Jesus, who with you and the Holy Spirit lives and reigns. **Amen.**

PROPER 16: *Sunday closest to August 24*

Loving God, we desire to serve you in sincerity and faithfulness; hear the prayers of your people and strengthen us for the work you have given us to do as we say, Lord in your mercy, hear our prayer.

Remember your holy church; that it might always be strong in the Lord and in the strength of your power.
Lord in your mercy, **hear our prayer.**

Guide our civic and political leaders; that they might make decisions and craft policies that benefit all people.
Lord in your mercy, **hear our prayer.**

Inspire the people of our local community; that this might be a place where people thrive and live in peace and neighborly good will.
Lord in your mercy, **hear our prayer.**

Touch the hearts of those who seek you and guide them here that they might encounter the living Christ among us.
Lord in your mercy, **hear our prayer.**

Grant us wisdom in our use of natural resources that we might bequeath to our children and grandchildren a sustainable and abundant world.
Lord in your mercy, **hear our prayer.**

Bring healing and wholeness to all who suffer in any way. [Especially we ask for...*prayer list.*]
Lord in your mercy, **hear our prayer.**

We trust in your care of those who have died; guide us so that our faith journeys might take us into your eternal kingdom.
Lord in your mercy, **hear our prayer.**

"Lord, to whom can we go? You have the words of eternal life. We have come to believe and know that you are the Holy One of God." Embolden and empower us to be vessels of your grace, and all these we ask through your Son, our Lord, Jesus Christ. **Amen.**

LECTIONARY YEAR B

PROPER 17: *Sunday closest to August 31*

Generous God, accept and answer our prayers as we say, Lord in your mercy, hear our prayer.

Keep your church humble and keep us ever mindful of our call to serve our neighbors with generous and loving hearts.
Lord in your mercy, **hear our prayer.**

Strengthen us that we might work together to demand justice and equity for all people in this nation and across the world.
Lord in your mercy, **hear our prayer.**

Enliven our faith that we might be doers of the Word and agents of your love to all whom we encounter.
Lord in your mercy, **hear our prayer.**

Show us how to be effective stewards and peacemakers that through us our world might be transformed and become a place where all people can thrive and live into their God-created potential.
Lord in your mercy, **hear our prayer.**

Care for the suffering, the sick, and all who know oppression and alienation, that they might know hope and be transformed by your peace.
[Especially we pray for…*prayer list.*]
Lord in your mercy, **hear our prayer.**

Grant all who have died the joy of your eternal presence and welcome us into the glorious life of your new age.
Lord in your mercy, **hear our prayer.**

We offer these prayers in the sure and certain hope of faith in your Son, Christ our Lord, who is our advocate and guide. **Amen.**

PROPER 18: *Sunday closest to September 7*

God calls us today to be open to the word and to one another. Let us open ourselves to all the world in prayer saying, Lord in your mercy, hear our prayer.

For the whole church we pray. That we may bring God's word of life to all who are in silence, darkness, or despair.
Lord in your mercy, **hear our prayer.**

For the world we pray. That nations will come to cooperate for the health and well-being of all,
Lord in your mercy, **hear our prayer.**

For our congregation we pray. That we may grow into the mystery of God's life among and in us,
Lord in your mercy, **hear our prayer.**

For our community we pray. That it might be a place of health, well-being, and personal dignity,
Lord in your mercy, **hear our prayer.**

For those suffering in any way we pray; especially for all who have asked for our prayers that they may know the healing power of God's love.
[For...*prayer list.*]
Lord in your mercy, **hear our prayer.**

For all mourners we pray. That all who grieve the coming of death may come to know life in the mercy of God.
Lord in your mercy, **hear our prayer.**

Into your mercy, O God, we commend all the needy world, trusting in your almighty power, through your Son, Jesus Christ, our Lord. **Amen.**

PROPER 19: *Sunday closest to September 14*

Let us cry out to the Lord with our prayers and petitions saying, Lord in your mercy, hear our prayer.

The Lord has given us the beauty of worship and the gift of fellowship with one another. We thank you Lord, for the church.
Lord in your mercy, **hear our prayer.**

The Lord has given us life in a nation of opportunities and liberty; with public services such as fire and police protection, ambulances, food pantries, schools, libraries, and hospitals.
We thank you Lord, for our national life.
Lord in your mercy, **hear our prayer.**

The Lord has given us neighbors, friends, families, and coworkers to share the joys and burdens of this life. We thank you Lord, for the privilege of loving others.
Lord in your mercy, **hear our prayer.**

The Lord has given us a world full of creatures that crawl, fly, swim, and climb. We enjoy a bounty of flowers and shrubs, grasses and trees, plants and moss, and rocks and hills. We thank you Lord, for your creation.
Lord in your mercy, **hear our prayer.**

The Lord has given us one another and we thank God for his grace and, offering for his mercy the sick and suffering. [We especially pray for… *prayer list.]*
Lord in your mercy, **hear our prayer.**

The Lord has given us a promise that where He goes, He will prepare a place for us. We thank you Lord for the gift of life and for giving us to one another for safekeeping. Bring us home when it is time.
Lord in your mercy, **hear our prayer.**

The Lord has given us permission to pray with the audacity of heirs and the openness of children. Thank you, Lord, for listening to us today. In Jesus name we pray. **Amen.**

PROPER 20: *Sunday closest to September 21*

Merciful Lord, hear us as we consider the needs of the world and your people as we pray, Lord in your mercy, hear our prayer.

We pray for your church in all places around the world and give you thanks that we share one faith and one hope that begins and ends with you.
Lord in your mercy, **hear our prayer.**

We pray for the needs of our nation, for those who live in states we have never seen, for those who face natural disasters we have not experienced and who we hope to serve in their time of need.
Lord in your mercy, **hear our prayer.**

We pray for this congregation. May we share one another's joys and burdens.
Lord in your mercy, **hear our prayer.**

We pray for those desperate for cures, those waiting for a miracle, those who need diagnosis and comfort and prayer. Deliver the sick from fear and pain, give sleep to the restless and comfort to those in need. [We pray especially for…*prayer list.*]
Lord in your mercy, **hear our prayer.**

We pray for the dying and those who sit at bedsides weeping. Bring comfort and deliverance, Lord, for our eternal rest is always in you.
Lord in your mercy, **hear our prayer.**

We ask these prayers in the name of our savior Jesus Christ who reigns with you and the holy spirit, one God everlasting. **Amen.**

PROPER 21: *Sunday closest to September 28*

God of peace, we offer ourselves, heart, and soul, and mind to you. Respond to our prayers as we say, Lord in your mercy **hear our prayer.**

Help your church to face the world with grace, humility, and love. Let us be a beacon of hope and a sanctuary of peace.
Lord in your mercy, **hear our prayer.**

Give your wisdom to the leaders of the nations that they might work together for the good of the whole world.
Lord in your mercy, **hear our prayer.**

Draw us close to you, that we might be renewed by your love and emboldened to carry out the ministry of Christ in our own community.
Lord in your mercy, **hear our prayer.**

Bestow upon us a reverence for your created world and hearts that ache to care for it.
Lord in your mercy, **hear our prayer.**

Wrap all who know pain or sickness into your healing embrace, give them courage and perseverance and remind them that you are with them in their suffering.
Lord in your mercy, **hear our prayer.**

Shower the dead with your love that they might be at peace and free from the tribulations of this life; and at the dawn of your new age, reunite us with those whom we love but are now beyond our reach.
Lord in your mercy, **hear our prayer.**

Almighty God, who was and is and is to come, bestow your blessings upon us and answer our prayers as may be best for us, and all this we ask through your Son, Jesus Christ, who is our redeemer and savior. **Amen.**

PROPER 22: *Sunday closest to October 5*

Creating and sustaining God, in faith we lift our voices to you that we might be transformed by your love saying, Lord in your mercy, hear our prayer.

We pray for the church, that it may manifest your grace and mercy in the world.
Lord in your mercy, **hear our prayer.**

We pray for our nation, that it might fulfill its promise and be a nation where people know justice, peace, and the opportunity to thrive.
Lord in your mercy, **hear our prayer.**

We pray for this assembly, that we might be a place where each of us can discover our call and find ways to minister together as the body of Christ.
Lord in your mercy, **hear our prayer.**

We pray for the natural order, that the abundance and diversity of creation might be preserved through our choices and advocacy.
Lord in your mercy, **hear our prayer.**

We pray for the sick, the injured, the anxious and despairing, grant them hope and wholeness through the power of your healing presence.
[Especially we lift up…*prayer list*.]
Lord in your mercy, **hear our prayer.**

We pray for the dead and the dying, that they might fulfill your will for them and rest in the glory of your eternal love.
Lord in your mercy, **hear our prayer.**

You have promised to hear and respond to us when we gather in your name; answer us with your loving kindness that our hopes may be fulfilled. All this we ask through the One who showed us your love most perfectly, Jesus Christ. **Amen.**

LECTIONARY YEAR B

PROPER 23: *Sunday closest to October 12*

God in three persons, hear us as we cry out in faith for the needs of your church universal, the clergy, the people, those served and those seeking you; praying, Lord in your mercy, hear our prayer.

Hear us as we cry out in hope for all that you are doing in our nation and in the hearts of those who serve. Bless us with peace and protect those who serve in our name.
Lord in your mercy, **hear our prayer.**

Hear us as we cry out in urgency for the needs of oppressed people everywhere, for the needs of the hungry, the poor, the unemployed, the homeless, the ill, the hopeless, the addicted, the incarcerated, the people in our homes and workplaces.
Lord in your mercy, **hear our prayer.**

Hear us as we cry out for the protection of our communities and all communities everywhere especially for the security of children, those in mental distress, the incarcerated and the elderly.
Lord in your mercy, **hear our prayer.**

Hear us we pray for ourselves and those who are ill. Restore each of us to good health in body, mind, and spirit. [Especially...*prayer list.*]
Lord in your mercy, **hear our prayer.**

Hear us as we pray for the dying, for a peaceful end and a certain faith.
Lord in your mercy, **hear our prayer.**

These prayers and petitions are offered in thanksgiving to you, O Lord, Father, Son and Holy Spriit, in full confidence that you will provide for us and for all in your time. **Amen.**

PROPER 24: *Sunday closest to October 19*

Abiding God, dwell with us and fulfill our desires as may be best for us as we say, Lord in your mercy, hear our prayer.

Give life to your church and to your people, strengthen us when we are weak, embolden us when we are afraid, and show us how to more perfectly embody your Son, Christ our Lord.
Lord in your mercy, **hear our prayer.**

Give peace to this nation and wisdom to its leaders; inspire them and us to work together to solve our problems and to bring opportunity for all to thrive.
Lord in your mercy, **hear our prayer.**

Give a stronger faith and more loving hearts to all of us gathered here today; let us be a blessing to our neighbors and a place of hope for all people.
Lord in your mercy, **hear our prayer.**

Give healing and wholeness to those who suffer in body, mind, or spirit. [Especially we ask on behalf of those who have sought our prayers, for... *prayer list.*]
Lord in your mercy, **hear our prayer.**

Give us courage and wisdom to identify and implement policies for a preserved environment and for a more equitable society.
Lord in your mercy, **hear our prayer.**

Give to the dead and dying eternal peace and comfort and give consolation and confidence in your promises to those who grieve.
Lord in your mercy, **hear our prayer.**

In Christ you have fulfilled your promises and set us free from the tyranny of sin, show us how to use our freedom to live more fully into your abundant life and to show the transforming power of your love to a world in need of hope and reconciliation. Through that same Christ we offer these prayers, who with you and the Holy Spirit, lives and reigns, now and always. **Amen.**

LECTIONARY YEAR B

PROPER 25: *Sunday closest to October 26*

Lord, you sent your Son to live among us so that we might know you better. Hear us now as we pray, Lord in your mercy, hear our prayer.

In your mercy, grant your church a true heart for the good news you give us in the words of scripture and in the Word made flesh, Jesus.
Lord in your mercy, **hear our prayer.**

In your mercy grant our nation a strong sense of service and an urgency to provide for all people. Especially bless our President, Vice-President, all those who serve the White House, the Congress, and Supreme Court with hearts that serve every citizen of this great country.
Lord in your mercy, **hear our prayer.**

In your mercy grant to all communities the things we need for true life – shelter, food, education, safety, and opportunity.
Lord in your mercy, **hear our prayer.**

In your mercy grant to our families and friends a sense of wonder at the world you created for us and that same sense of gratitude for all the people who you created to serve this world.
Lord in your mercy, **hear our prayer.**

In your mercy, grant health and healing for our relationships with you, with our families and friends. Mend broken hearts and give us pathways to reconciliation.
Lord in your mercy, **hear our prayer.**

In your mercy bless the sick and suffering with healing. [We pray especially for...*prayer list.*]
Lord in your mercy, **hear our prayer.**

In your mercy receive the dying into your loving arms and grant them a new life in your kingdom. Comfort those who mourn and bring them into deeper relationship with you.
Lord in your mercy, hear our prayer.

We ask this in the name of the One God in three persons, Father, Son, and Holy Spirit. We praise you and bless you, this day and always. **Amen.**

PROPER 26: *Sunday closest to November 2*

God of hope, so that your will for us might be complete, respond to the prayers of your people and answer our hopes and needs as we say, Lord in your mercy, hear our prayer.

That your people across the world might set aside their differences and learn to work as one for the sake of the gospel mission to love our neighbors, we pray.
Lord in your mercy, **hear our prayer.**

That this nation might be an advocate for peace and liberty and an example of justice and opportunity to the whole world, we pray.
Lord in your mercy, **hear our prayer.**

That this assembly might grow in faith and love and find new ways to truly love and serve our neighbors, we pray.
Lord in your mercy, **hear our prayer.**

That our climate challenges might be answered with courage and determination, and the abundance of your natural world preserved, we pray.
Lord in your mercy, **hear our prayer.**

That those challenged by sickness or injury might be made whole and know the healing peace of Christ which passes all understanding, we pray.
Lord in your mercy, **hear our prayer.**

That the dying might enter into your eternal embrace and that we too may join with all your saints in your new kingdom, we pray.
Lord in your mercy, **hear our prayer.**

Help us to marshal our whole selves in service to your Good News and expand our perception that we might fully know the abundant life of Christ throughout our lives. We ask this through that same Christ, our only advocate and Lord. **Amen.**

LECTIONARY YEAR B

PROPER 27: *Sunday closest to November 9*

Let us pray for the needs of the world, calling to our loving God, Lord in your mercy, hear our prayer.

Lord, you called the widow generous and spurned the gifts of those who gave to you only to be deemed holy by others. Give us hearts of generosity that seek ways to give to your church, your missionaries, your people in need, and in lavish delight to those most in need.
Lord in your mercy, **hear our prayer.**

Lord, give to our national and community leaders a desire to give generously of their time, their talents, their ideas, and their faith. Remind every person in authority that leadership requires a generous spirit but even more, a generous heart.
Lord in your mercy, **hear our prayer.**

Lord, give to those who are anxious this day, a sense of your nearness, that they might feel your comfort. Ease our burdens and worries, give us peace and patience and a way forward.
Lord in your mercy, **hear our prayer.**

Lord, give to us a reverence for your creation and a keen desire protect and advocate for the preservation and sustenance of the natural world.
Lord in your mercy, **hear our prayer.**

Lord, bless those who are facing long term illness, loss of independence, diagnosis and testing, a hope that, in you, all things are made new, and no life is insignificant in your eyes. We pray for all those who are in need of our prayers. [Especially...*prayer list.*]
Lord in your mercy, **hear our prayer.**

Lord, give to the dying your peace and comfort and bring them to abide with you in your heavenly kingdom.
Lord in your mercy, **hear our prayer.**

Gracious God, thank you for hearing our prayers. Use us in our turn, to help fulfill the prayers and needs of others. In Jesus name, **Amen.**

PROPER 28: *Sunday closest to November 16*

Holy God, you have shown us your love and steadfastness in the power of your promises. We offer our prayers through our Lord and High Priest, Jesus Christ who is our only mediator and advocate saying, Lord in your mercy, hear our prayer.

For the church, that it might faithfully answer your call and eagerly do the work you have given us to do,
Lord in your mercy, **hear our prayer.**

For the leaders of our nation and of all nations, that they might value the greater good and promote the flourishing of all people.
Lord in your mercy, **hear our prayers.**

For the welfare of our world, that we might be wise stewards of God's abundance in creation.
Lord in your mercy, **hear our prayer.**

For all in our community who are experiencing joblessness, hunger, indifference, homelessness, and all the ways that basic human dignity is undermined.
Lord in your mercy, **hear our prayer.**

For all who are suffering and in need of healing. [Especially for… *prayer list.*]
Lord in your mercy, **hear our prayer.**

For all those who have died, for those in our hearts and those unknown or forgotten; that their memories may be held close by God until that day when all are restored in the next age.
Lord in your mercy, **hear our prayer.**

Hear us O Lord, be our guide and strength to answer our fears and hopes as may be best for us and for your greater glory; all this we ask through Jesus, your Son, who lives and reigns with you and the Holy Spirit, One God, now and always. **Amen.**

Proper 29: CHRIST THE KING *Sunday Closest to November 23*

Marvelous, glorious God, with sincere thanks for the blessings won by Christ our Lord, we offer to you our deepest prayers as we say, Lord in your mercy, hear our prayer.

May your Church always look to its head, the Lord Jesus, whose example has given us a template for our lives and commission calls us forward in mission and ministry.
Lord in your mercy, **hear our prayer.**

Strengthen us to be advocates for justice and peace in our society, that the reign of Christ might be known in our nation's life.
Lord in your mercy, **hear our prayer.**

Be present to us today so that, with confidence in Christ's promises, we might re-commit ourselves to lives of service in His name and become agents of God's love to all whom we encounter.
Lord in your mercy, **hear our prayer.**

You have formed the creation that it might sustain us and help us to thrive, help us to use it responsibly and to work with others to sustain its bounty.
Lord in your mercy, **hear our prayer.**

The name of Christ is the only name given for health under heaven, let His healing power enter into the lives of all who suffer that they may be made whole and know peace. [Especially we pray for…*prayer list.*]
Lord in your mercy, **hear our prayer.**

Welcome the dead into your glorious eternal presence, that with the saints and angels they may praise you on your throne.
Lord in your mercy, **hear our prayer.**

King of kings and Lord of Lords, you are our one true allegiance, and we give thanks for your reign. So lead us that we might welcome your return in confidence and hope. We offer these prayers in the name of Christ the King, who with the Father and the Holy Spirit lives and reigns forever. **Amen.**

Lectionary Year C

FIRST SUNDAY OF ADVENT

Faithful God, we offer our prayers in hopeful anticipation of your response as we say, Lord in your mercy, hear our prayer.

Your church waits in anticipation for the fulfillment of your promises, grant us perseverance and urgency to continue Christ's mission as we await His return.
Lord in your mercy, **hear our prayer.**

Sow the seeds of your love throughout this nation, that our people and leaders might work towards building a society where all people have an equitable place and the opportunity to thrive.
Lord in your mercy, **hear our prayer.**

As we enter into this season of anticipation, grant this congregation a discerning spirit that we might confidently follow where you are leading us, be beacons of hope, and a place of refuge for our neighbors.
Lord in your mercy, **hear our prayer.**

Your creation cries out from the devastation wrought by our unsustainable use of its resources, show us how we might change and advocate for a holy stewardship of the natural world.
Lord in your mercy, **hear our prayer.**

Open our hearts to know the suffering of those who are sick, afraid, alone, or oppressed; grant them relief, healing, and wholeness and show us how to be present with them. [Especially we ask for those who have sought our prayers…*prayer list.*]
Lord in your mercy, **hear our prayer.**

Grant to the dying peace and rest in your loving care; and grant to us and them an entrance into the resurrected life of Christ.
Lord in your mercy, **hear our prayer.**

Hear the hopes and needs of your people and respond; keep your people in your grace just as you always have. Through our Lord, Jesus Christ, who with you and the Holy Spirit lives reigns. **Amen.**

SECOND SUNDAY OF ADVENT

Holy God, wherever we are, you are there. Stir our hearts wherever we may go that we may see you and offer thanksgiving for the life you have given us. Hear these prayers we offer as we say, Lord in your mercy, hear our prayer.

For the church in every place: May we be ever mindful of the richness of the family of the God's people, those next to us here, those in neighborhood churches, and those worshipping today across the globe. Help us to grow into a unity of mission and ministry in our common devotion to Christ that we might be faithful witnesses of your love.
Lord in your mercy, **hear our prayer.**

For those in civil authority: That they be guided by hope and not fear.
Lord in your mercy, **hear our prayer.**

For this faith community; amid joys and sorrows: Let us remember those who have gone before us; those who have sacrificed for us. Let us give thanks for this gathering of God's people and for the renewal of life we are given.
Lord in your mercy, **hear our prayer.**

For the gifts of creation, for the sun that lights our day and the moon and stars that shelter the night: May our eyes be open to the beauty around us. Help us to protect and nurture the creation and ever proclaim its wonders.
Lord in your mercy, **hear our prayer.**

For those at greatest risk among us: Let us pray for those who are lonely or neglected, and for those facing illness and disability. [Especially we pray for...*prayer list.*]
Lord in your mercy, **hear our prayer.**

For those who have died, for those who are dying, and for those who grieve, that they might find hope in your promise of lasting life.
Lord in your mercy, **hear our prayer.**

Lord, gather up our prayers with those of all your people in every place and time, and guide us to Christ, preparing the way for us by making every valley filled and every mountain low. **Amen.**

LECTIONARY YEAR C

THIRD SUNDAY OF ADVENT

Let our hearts and minds be stirred as we pray to God for the peace that passes understanding, and rejoice in the gift of Christ, saying, Lord in your mercy, hear our prayer.

For peace in the church: May we intensify our efforts at peace-making with the separated churches, that peace may prevail over conflict, and that we may be reconciled into one family, exercising one baptism, one eucharist, and one common ministry in its many forms.
Lord in your mercy, **hear our prayer.**

For peace in the world: May conflicts cease, may refugees and survivors find new homes and the spirit to begin again. May wounds be healed, losses grieved, and honorable deeds remembered. May grace abound in all lands and may the lion and the lamb lie content.
Lord in your mercy, **hear our prayer.**

For this assembly. That the world might know us by our love. Help us with the grievances we harbor within our families and communities and among our co-workers and friends. Help us build trust and teach us forgiveness that we might know reconciliation in your love.
Lord in your mercy, **hear our prayer.**

For peace where we live, work and play, and for peace within ourselves: May the noises in and around us diminish so that we can hear the quiet sounds of Creation. And grant us time and space to listen for you, our heart's true desire.
Lord in your mercy, **hear our prayer.**

For all those who suffer, may we be messengers of hope, peace, and healing. [Especially we pray for all those who have sought our prayers, for.... *prayer list.*]
Lord in your mercy, **hear our prayer.**

For those who are gone and beyond our reach, fill the empty spots in our hearts and souls with reassurance of your love for them and fill them also with the hope of our reuniting someday in your eternal kingdom.
Lord in your mercy, **hear our prayer.**

O Lord, fill our minds and hearts with everything that is good and loving and worthy of thanksgiving and praise, everything that comes to us under the sign of your peace and in the name of Christ our Lord. **Amen.**

FOURTH SUNDAY OF ADVENT

May our hearts leap for joy as we again assemble in prayer to await the Lord's coming. With Mary, may our souls proclaim God's greatness as we say, Lord in your mercy, **hear our prayer.**

Let us pray for the church: As the celebration of your incarnation draws near, we remember the many ways your revelation is lifted up in the world and we pray for our sisters and brothers in Christ throughout the world, and especially for those whose very faith endangers their lives.
Lord in your mercy, **hear our prayer.**

For an end to violence, oppression, and injustice: As you lead us, Lord, from darkness to light, may we be among those who exalt the lowly and fill the hungry with good things, rooting out the proud of heart and drawing courage from the power of your arm.
Lord in your mercy, **hear our prayer.**

For our own spirits: May our hearts be magnified and made much bigger than we think possible. May this season of Advent stir in us such faith that we exert ourselves to be your light in a darkened world.
Lord in your mercy, **hear our prayer.**

For this community: May we be enriched by welcoming the stranger and be drawn to a bright future in service to you, while also remembering and honoring those in the past who guided us into faith.
Lord in your mercy, **hear our prayer.**

For the sick and suffering. May they find healing and peace. [Especially we pray for…*prayer list*]
Lord in your mercy, **hear our prayer.**

For the dead and those on the threshold of death. May they and we be welcomed into the place of glory our Lord has prepared for us.
Lord in your mercy, **hear our prayer.**

Lord, we gather up the prayers of this household, confident in your promise to be with us always. Guide us in wisdom and faith; that we might live into the life created for us, trusting in your will. All this we ask through your Son, our redeemer, Jesus, who is your Christ. **Amen.**

FIRST SUNDAY AFTER CHRISTMAS

Let us pray for ourselves and the world saying, Lord in your mercy, hear our prayer.

Heavenly Father, your love spoke the world into existence and abides with us still. Give your church the hunger to know you, the will to study you, and the heart to be your action in the world.
Lord in your mercy, **hear our prayer.**

Lord of all nations, bless this nation and all nations this coming year with peace and abundance. May we find new ways of being together in service for the common good.
Lord in your mercy, **hear our prayer.**

Lord of all light, make this a season of good news for all those in the world who are persecuted and bereaved.
Lord in your mercy, **hear our prayer.**

Lord who is constant, grant healing to those who suffer from anxiety and depression, from disease and illness and from all manner of things that affect our body, mind, and spirit. [We pray especially for... *prayer list.*]
Lord in your mercy, **hear our prayer.**

Lord deliver all the dying into the comfort of your eternal kingdom, where suffering is gone and where love and restoration are found.
Lord in your mercy, **hear our prayer.**

In thanksgiving to you for the love with which you have formed the world, its creatures and us your people; we end our prayers with the hope of living this life in deep awareness of you, O Father; you, O Son and you, Most Holy Spirit. **Amen.**

SECOND SUNDAY AFTER CHRISTMAS

As we continue our rejoicing in the incarnation of Christ, let us lift up our prayers to God asking humbly for God's mercy and grace saying, Lord in your mercy, hear our prayer.

For the people of God throughout the world; that our joy in Christ's presence might inspire our unity in mission as the undivided body of Christ.
Lord in your mercy, **hear our prayer.**

For the nation and those holding civil authority; that they might exercise their authority with wisdom and equity, seeking to serve only the common good.
Lord in your mercy, **hear our prayer.**

For our local communities, that we might endeavor to make them places where we and our neighbors can live with dignity and purpose.
Lord in your mercy, **hear our prayer.**

For the natural world, the vehicle of God's abundance; that we might be effective stewards and ceaseless advocates for its sustainability.
Lord in your mercy, **hear our prayer.**

For those in our lives who are suffering and in distress; that Christ's healing presence might be made manifest in their lives. [Especially we pray for...*prayer list*.]
Lord in your mercy, **hear our prayer.**

For those who have died; that they may rest in your loving care and that we may be reunited with them in the coming age.
Lord in your mercy, **hear our prayer.**

Loving God, who hears our cries and knows our needs before we are even aware of them; answer our prayers and lead us into goodness and light that we might be your people and the body of Christ. **Amen.**

FIRST SUNDAY AFTER EPIPHANY

Glorious and Wondrous God, in thankfulness and confidence we lift our hopes and needs to you in prayer as we say, Lord in your mercy, hear our prayer.

Raise up in your church leaders whose lives are centered in the love of Christ and whose hearts yearn for justice and peace.
Lord in your mercy, **hear our prayer.**

Enter into the hearts of those with authority in our nation that they might work for the fellowship of all people and bring about a world where enemies are reconciled and conflict ceases.
Lord in your mercy, **hear our prayer.**

Inspire this assembly through the inbreaking of the Spirit in our lives that our faiths may be bolstered and our commitment to the gospel mission renewed.
Lord in your mercy, **hear our prayer.**

Instill in us awe and thankfulness for the majesty of your created world that we might be good stewards and develop sustainable practices so that nature's abundance might be available to all future generations.
Lord in your mercy, **hear our prayer.**

Bring healing to the sick and hurting, mend the fractured and broken, grant hope to the fearful and anxious, and grant peace and the knowledge of your love to all people. [Especially we pray for…*prayer list.*]
Lord in your mercy, **hear our prayer.**

Grant to the faithful departed peace and rest in your eternal love and, welcome us into the resurrection alongside all your saints.
Lord in your mercy, **hear our prayer.**

Hear our prayers and grant our desires as may be best for us and in ways that show forth your grace and mercy. All this we ask through our only advocate and Lord, Jesus, who is Christ and lives with you and the Holy Spirit, one God, forever and ever. **Amen.**

SECOND SUNDAY AFTER EPIPHANY

Gathering our hearts and minds, let us offer God the words of our hearts, saying Lord in your mercy, hear our prayer.

We pray for the church, pray for those who serve, those who pray, those who fear to enter its doors.
Lord in your mercy, **hear our prayer.**

We pray for our own clergy, for our bishop(s), priests and deacons, for our lay leaders and ministers and all who seek to follow God.
Lord in your mercy, **hear our prayer.**

We pray for our communities. Pray for those who work late shifts and long hours, for those who have no possibility of employment; for those who hunger for food and connection; for those who respond to emergencies and those who keep doors open.
Lord in your mercy, **hear our prayer.**

We pray for the needs of all the world's people; for good and strong leaders and for responsive politicians to turn their energies and hearts toward solutions providing lasting peace, adequate resources, and safety for all people.
Lord in your mercy, **hear our prayer.**

We pray for those who are anxious and depressed; for those who are addicted and weary; for those who are sick and suffering; for those who are waiting for diagnosis and those who are living with diagnosis. [Pray especially for…*prayer list*.]
Lord in your mercy, **hear our prayer.**

We pray for the dying; pray for those who wait to meet their savior and for those who mourn the loss of them. Bring all souls into the loving embrace of your angels and into the light of your kingdom.
Lord in your mercy, **hear our prayer.**

We offer all these prayers with confidence in you, O Father of all; and you O Son who came among us; and you O Spirit who flows in us and the world. **Amen.**

LECTIONARY YEAR C

THIRD SUNDAY AFTER EPIPHANY

Marvelous God who has brought forth many wonderful works, hear our prayers and answer our needs and hopes as we pray, Lord in your mercy, hear our prayer.

Help your church to see its strength in openness and cooperation, help us to forge bonds of mission and ministry with others that your glory might extend across the whole earth.
Lord in your mercy, **hear our prayer.**

Let the light of truth and justice shine forth across our nation; may this nation be a place of peace and opportunity for all its people.
Lord in your mercy, **hear our prayer.**

Send your Spirit upon this assembly that this might be place of refuge, a beacon of hope, and a true embodiment of the Good News for our neighbors.
Lord in your mercy, **hear our prayer.**

May your holy words guide us in our endeavor to be good stewards of your good creation, ensuring its abundance for ourselves and for those yet to be born.
Lord in your mercy, **hear our prayer.**

Lift up the lowly and forgotten, gather the marginalized, and bring liberty to the oppressed that the power of your love might inspire all people.
Lord in your mercy, **hear our prayer.**

Bring your healing spirit to bear in the lives of all who suffer from any sickness or infirmity. Let them know wholeness, wellness, and peace.
[Especially we pray for…*prayer list.*]
Lord in your mercy, **hear our prayer.**

Receive the dying into your loving arms eternally; may we and they some day know you face to face in your coming age.
Lord in your mercy, **hear our prayer.**

Hear the prayers of your people and answer us as you have answered your people across time so that we might feel your presence among us and strengthen us for the call of being agents of your love in the world. **Amen.**

FOURTH SUNDAY AFTER EPIPHANY

Let us pray to the Lord who enlightens the nations and gives us hope by praying, Lord in your mercy, hear our prayer.

The church has a mission to light the nations with love and hope. Lord, send us out to do your will.
Lord in your mercy, **hear our prayer.**

Our nation has resources and abundance like no other country Lord. Show us the way to share what we have with our own brothers and sisters in the United States and to help our neighbors around the world.
Lord in your mercy, **hear our prayer.**

Our world was a gift from you, and we are the stewards of your creation. Give us wisdom to conserve and protect all that you have made.
Lord in your mercy, **hear our prayer.**

Our community has the problems of homelessness, hunger, poverty, injustice, unemployment, and loneliness. Give us the courage to address them as a church and as your disciples.
Lord in your mercy, **hear our prayer.**

Our friends and families are in need of healing. Give your grace, peace, protection, and healing to those we offer to you now. [Especially we pray for...*prayer list.*]
Lord in your mercy, **hear our prayer.**

Our life ends with new life in you. Bless the dying with peace and the grieving with comfort.
Lord in your mercy, **hear our prayer.**

Our lives and wellbeing are held in your hand O Lord. Give us trust and faith in you and bless us this day and every day with the peace that only you provide. In the name of the Father, the Son, and the Holy Spirit. **Amen.**

FIFTH SUNDAY AFTER EPIPHANY

God of promises, we come before you, acknowledging our limitations, but also giving voice to our hopes and needs that your promises might live within us, offering the desires of our hearts as we say, Lord in your mercy hear our prayer.

We pray for the people of God, called to witness and to serve; that we might persevere in taking up and continuing Jesus' own earthly ministries. Lord in your mercy, **hear our prayer.**

We pray for those holding the authority of governance over us; that you might inspire and lead them to always choose the greatest good and to respect the dignity of all people.
Lord in your mercy, **hear our prayer.**

We pray for all the places we make our homes; that they might be places where the gospel is known and followed and that we might be powerful icons of your love.
Lord in your mercy, **hear our prayer.**

We pray for the created world, for the right and sustainable uses of the earth's resources; that all generations might know your intended abundance.
Lord in your mercy, **hear our prayer.**

We pray for all who suffer and all who tend to their needs; let your healing presence be manifest in their lives. [We pray especially for…*prayer list*.]
Lord in your mercy hear our prayer.

We pray for all who have died and for those who grieve. Keep them in your care and let us all rise together in your new age.
Lord in your mercy, **hear our prayer.**

Almighty God, your steadfastness and devotion are beyond our understanding. Help us to see your works in our midst and to accept your invitation to abundant life, and all these we ask through your beloved, Christ Jesus, who with you and the Holy Spirit lives and reign, world without end. **Amen.**

SIXTH SUNDAY AFTER EPIPHANY

Let us pray, turning our hearts toward the one who makes our desert hearts bloom with the flowers of hope saying, Lord in your mercy, hear our prayer.

Engrave our hearts with your living word of love, that we might listen and turn to you.
Lord in your mercy, **hear our prayer.**

Deepen the life of your church, giving it a will to serve the world in your name, and a spirit of welcome that draws all those who hunger to your table.
Lord in your mercy, **hear our prayer.**

Give your blessing of courage and truth to those who hold authority in our cities, towns, states, and countries and to those who hold authority in our churches, workplaces, and lives.
Lord in your mercy, **hear our prayer.**

The world cries out in despair and desolation. Send your love to heal the brokenness that has become a desert placc in our time.
Lord in your mercy, **hear our prayer.**

Quench the thirst of those who long for healing, cure, and reconciliation. Be with those who suffer in body, mind, and spirit, and comfort those who anxiously await a word of hope. [Especially we pray for *prayer list*.]
Lord in your mercy, **hear our prayer.**

Bring your promise of life in fullness to those who struggle, to those who are oppressed and persecuted, and to those in any kind of need.
Lord in your mercy, **hear our prayer.**

Hold in your care those who have died and welcome us into your eternal arms when our time comes, and let us all rise together in your new age.
Lord in your mercy, **hear our prayer.**

In the hope of the life to come and in communion with those who have died, we look to the day where with your son and the Holy Spirit we might come to dwell in your verdant kingdom. **Amen.**

SEVENTH SUNDAY AFTER EPIPHANY

Sustaining God, you have promised to turn our hearts from stone to flesh; to give us life through the power of your love and hear our hopes and needs. Answer these prayers lifted to you as we say, Lord in your mercy, hear our prayer.

For the people of God everywhere, that they me be beacons of hope whose light shines forth to dispel fear and hate.
Lord in your mercy, **hear our prayer.**

For those with authority over our lives, that they might wield their power for the common good and with respect for the dignity of all people.
Lord in your mercy, **hear our prayer.**

For those in our lives who have caused us pain and hurt; lead them to an awareness of their impact and lead us to the path of forgiveness where those hurts have no hold on us.
Lord in your mercy, **hear our prayer.**

For our local communities - our neighbors, our co-workers, and our classmates, help us to sow the seeds of your kingdom in our daily interactions.
Lord in your mercy, **hear our prayer.**

For our beleaguered earth, the garden where you have placed us; grant us wisdom as we discern how to be worthy stewards of this gift and give us strength and courage to persevere in its preservation.
Lord in your mercy, **hear our prayer.**

For all who live in pain, in sickness, in fear or dread; sustain them with your grace that they might bear their suffering and grant us an awareness and a willingness to be their companions and caregivers. [Especially we pray for...*prayer list.*]
Lord in your mercy, **hear our prayer.**

Hold in your care those who have died and welcome us into your eternal arms when our time comes, and let us all rise together in your new age.
Lord in your mercy, **hear our prayer.**
Almighty God who is the Sower of love, mercy, and hope; let us be the seeds of your salvation; growing in love ourselves that through us your hopeful mercy might be known and established everywhere, and hear our prayers, those spoken and those held quietly in our hearts that we might know grace and live into the people we were created to be. All this we ask through Christ, our Lord. **Amen.**

EIGHTH SUNDAY AFTER EPIPHANY

Saving God, answer the cries of our hearts as may be best for us and for the knowledge of your glorious love as we say, Lord in your mercy, hear our prayer.

We pray for the people of God across the world, that they may be steadfast in faith, strong in pursuit of justice, and persistent in seeking reconciliation.
Lord in your mercy, **hear our prayer.**

We pray for our nation and its leaders, grant them wisdom and discerning hearts to pursue peace and to create policies of opportunity and equity at home and across the globe.
Lord in your mercy, **hear our prayer.**

We pray for this community of faith, bring us closer to one another and show us how to be good neighbors that we might bear good fruit for the sake of the gospel.
Lord in your mercy, **hear our prayer.**

We pray for the earth and for the natural world, that it might be healed and restored to the full abundance with which you created it.
Lord in your mercy, **hear our prayer.**

We pray for all who know sickness, injury, anxiety, and fear. May your healing Spirit infiltrate their lives and bring them peace and restoration.
Lord in your mercy, **hear our prayer.**

We pray for the dead and dying, that your will for them may be made complete and that they may join in the chorus of praise which surrounds you.
Lord in your mercy, **hear our prayer.**

Wondrous God, whose promises beckon us forward into the heavenly light, hear and answer your people's prayers and fulfill in us the purpose with which you created us. And all this we ask through Him who has offered us salvation, Jesus Christ, who lives and reigns forever with you and the Holy Spirit. **Amen.**

LAST SUNDAY AFTER EPIPHANY

Led by the Holy Spirit we pray for the church and the world, saying, Lord in your mercy, hear our prayer.

For the church in all its guises, in every land and in every language, may your Word be known.
Lord in your mercy, **hear our prayer.**

For all who seek to follow Christ Jesus, that they may be steadfast in their love and faith and that they may work together for greater unity as Christ's body,
Lord in your mercy, **hear our prayer.**

For peace in all places and in the hearts of all people throughout the earth,
Lord in your mercy, **hear our prayer.**

For our community, especially for those struggling in economic transitions, that we might find strength and hope together.
Lord in your mercy, **hear our prayer.**

For the natural world and its abundance, that we might use that abundance wisely and sustainably.
Lord in your mercy, **hear our prayer.**

For all who are suffering, that they might find solace in your presence and wholeness in your love. [Especially for...*prayer list.*]
Lord in your mercy, **hear our prayer.**

For the saints in every generation, that their lives might inspire ours and that we might be faithful stewards of their legacy,
Lord in your mercy, **hear our prayer.**

God of wisdom and love, hear the prayers of your beloved children in this community of faith. Bring your help to all in need, granting our prayer through Christ our Lord. **Amen.**

FIRST SUNDAY IN LENT

In this, the first Sunday of the holy season of Lent, let us offer to God the deepest needs of our hearts crying out to him, Lord in your mercy, hear our prayer.

Holy One, bless this church with an ever-deepening faith and lead us forward in our own season of wonder as we prepare for the season of Lent.
Lord in your mercy, **hear our prayer.**

Holy One, bless those who hunger for your love. May we worship you in the beauty of holiness so that we may be strengthened and sent out into the world to serve your gospel.
Lord in your mercy, **hear our prayer.**

Holy One, bless our nation's leaders at all levels with wisdom, courtesy, compassion, and grace. Bless all who live here with a care for one another and a willingness to compromise.
Lord in your mercy, **hear our prayer.**

Holy One, protect the children and families of our community. Give them the gift of time, health, and love of you. Let us be a part of the life of families and especially send us to love the lonely and forgotten who live among us.
Lord in your mercy, **hear our prayer.**

Holy One, healing is one of our greatest needs in this life. It is our privilege to offer to you those we know who are in need of your healing and who seek a relief from pain and suffering. [We especially offer to you… *prayer list.*]
Lord in your mercy, **hear our prayer.**

Holy One, we know that you have prepared a place for us. Gather those who die in the light of your love and bless the grieving with comfort and peace.
Lord in your mercy, **hear our prayer.**

Holy God, Father, Son, and Holy Spirit, bless our prayers with your discerning love and lead us ever more into a deeper life of faith life with you. **Amen.**

SECOND SUNDAY IN LENT

Lord God, you gather us to you as your children and bid us this Lent to repent and turn to you. Hear our cries for mercy and turn our hearts of stone toward you as we pray, Lord in your mercy, hear our prayer.

Give us a heart for your church, give us ears that hear your call to worship and open our minds to the power of our parish community. Make your church a place of welcome, refuge, and relentless love.
Lord in your mercy, **hear our prayer.**

Shed your grace on those who govern and lead in every nation, state, city, and community. Turn those who have authority away from self-interest and toward the imperative of service and mercy.
Lord in your mercy, **hear our prayer.**

Strengthen the persecuted, comfort the oppressed, inspire those who chafe against injustice and cruelty that we might bring your kingdom goals of justice and mercy into the here and now.
Lord in your mercy, **hear our prayer.**

Restore those who suffer in body, mind, or spirit. Uphold the ill with your healing grace. [Especially we pray for…*prayer list.*]
Lord in your mercy, **hear our prayer.**

Give to the departed eternal rest and the joy of your kingdom's light and life. Secure the grieving in the knowledge of your unending love, and unite us at last when we dwell with you in eternal life.
Lord in your mercy, **hear our prayer.**

Holy God, Father, Son, and Holy Spirit, we offer our prayers and petitions to you, secure in the knowledge of your willingness to hear us and your delight when we do so. Grant our prayers to our benefit and always to your glory. **Amen.**

THIRD SUNDAY IN LENT

Loving God who is our refuge and our strength; hear us we beg you; listen to our words and the longings of our hearts as we turn to you in prayer, saying, Lord in your mercy, hear our prayer.

Give strength to your people across the whole earth, that we may be the lights of the world in our generations.
Lord in your mercy, **hear our prayer.**

Give mercy to those in authority over us that they might be leaders in service to the well-being of all people.
Lord in your mercy, **hear our prayer.**

Give hope and courage to this congregation, that together, we might be bold and courageous in taking up Christ's ministries as our own.
Lord in your mercy, **hear our prayer.**

Give wisdom and determination to us and to all people, so that we might create a sustainable future for the equitable use of the abundance of creation.
Lord in your mercy, **hear our prayer.**

Give wholeness to those bent and broken by sickness, pain, fear, oppression, or abuse, that they might hold on to their own dignity as your beloved children. [Especially we pray for ...*prayer list.*]
Lord in your mercy, **hear our prayer.**

Give comfort to those who grieve and care to those who have died, and grant that we might all know resurrected life in your new age.
Lord in your mercy, **hear our prayer.**

God of creation and salvation; you have promised to answer when we knock. We offer these prayers and all the intentions of our own hearts in the confidence of your promises, and we ask these through our advocate and Lord, Christ Jesus. **Amen.**

FOURTH SUNDAY IN LENT

Forgiving Father, you watch for us with a loving heart, welcoming us home to you. Give us the grace to see our path clearly and correct our course when we are led astray. Hear and answer our prayers to you as we say, Lord in your mercy, hear our prayer.

Send your message of love to the world through us, that we might be examples of your good news to those who know us. Use our hearts and hands to your purpose. Open our mouths to advocate for the poor. Give us ears that hear the cries of the lonely, the forgotten, the imprisoned, and the poor.
Lord in your mercy, **hear our prayer.**

Turn our foolish hearts from hate and division and unite us in a bond of love that will not tolerate persecution, violence, or waste. Give our leaders the desire for true service to your people and a passion for bringing peace to all nations.
Lord in your mercy, **hear our prayer.**

Give strength to those who are afraid, to those who are facing diagnoses, disaster, or loss. Comfort them with your spirit of hope and restore those things which have been lost.
Lord in your mercy, **hear our prayer.**

Turn us away from bitterness and hopelessness. Give healing to those who are ill, peace to those of anxious heart or defeated spirit, that they might find wholeness of body, mind, and soul. [Especially we pray for… *prayer list.*]
Lord in your mercy, **hear our prayer.**

Give comfort to those who grieve and care to those who have died, and grant that we might all know resurrected life in your new age.
Lord in your mercy, **hear our prayer.**

Father, you rejoice when what is lost becomes found in you; search our hearts and keep them ever focused on the abundant life we find in you, your Son and in the Holy Spirit. **Amen.**

FIFTH SUNDAY IN LENT

Forgiving God, hear and respond to us as we say, Lord in your mercy, hear our prayer.

Soften the hearts of your people, show us how to bear our calling with humility and grace, that together we may truly be the body of Christ for the world.
Lord in your mercy, **hear our prayer.**

Raise up leaders among us who are grounded in honesty, compassion, and selflessness, that they may guide our nation into fulfilling its promise, creating a nation where all have the opportunity to live into their potential.
Lord in your mercy, **hear our prayer.**

Bless this assembly and help us to see more clearly our bonds to one another and the ways you have called us to serve our community together.
Lord in your mercy, **hear our prayer.**

Restore the abundant and protective glory of nature and embolden us to be advocates for and stewards of your created world.
Lord in your mercy, **hear our prayer.**

Bring your healing powers to bear on all who suffer, give knowledge and skill to those in healing vocations, and empower us to be servants to those in any need. [Especially we pray for…*prayer list.*]
Lord in your mercy, **hear our prayer.**

Greet the dying with love and welcome, grant them an entrance into your holy presence and raise them up in your new age.
Lord in your mercy, **hear our prayer.**

Grant us these prayers Almighty God, through the love shown us by your Son, our Lord, Jesus Christ, who with your Holy Spirit are one God, indivisible and eternal. **Amen.**

SUNDAY OF THE PASSION: PALM SUNDAY

Like the followers of Jesus before us, we often fail to recognize His claim on our lives. Let us bow together and offer Him our fealty and our prayers saying, Lord in your mercy, hear our prayer

Open our hearts to see you as you draw near to us in our daily lives. Give us eyes that see your truth and hands that open to you in welcome, and give us the will to live this week with you in your journey from triumphant king to crucified messiah. Help us to carve out time to worship fully this holy week.
Lord in your mercy, **hear our prayer.**

Send the imperative of love into the leadership of all nations that we might move forward in finding lasting peace.
Lord in your mercy, **hear our prayer.**

Make us living banners of welcome to those who fear rejection and to those who experience disconnection from you and your church. Draw those who need you most into the circle of a supportive and welcoming congregation.
Lord in your mercy, **hear our prayer.**

Give us hands that reach out to the poor and suffering with food, clothing, shelter, and companionship. Give us your heart that we might walk the way of love.
Lord in your mercy, **hear our prayer.**

Heal the body, mind, and spirit of those who suffer with illness and despair. Bring hope and wellness to all your people. [We pray especially for… *prayer list.*]
Lord in your mercy, **hear our prayer.**

Gather the dying to you and relieve those who grieve. Keep us mindful of the promise that we might abide with you now and in the world to come.
Lord in your mercy, **hear our prayer.**

God of love and God of suffering, send your spirit to us now that we might companion with you in this special week of worship that leads us to the cross. Unite us to one another in your Son, Christ our Lord. **Amen.**

MAUNDY THURDAY

Hear us O God as you have promised and respond as may be best for us as we lift our voices in prayer saying, Lord in your mercy, hear our prayer.

May your church be a sacrament to the world, showing forth your love to the world, strengthened by the Holy Spirit, and led by the teachings and example of our Lord, Jesus Christ.
Lord in your mercy, **hear our prayer.**

May our nation be blessed with leaders who serve with humility and the desire to work on behalf of all.
Lord in your mercy, **hear our prayer.**

May your creation be healed of the damage we have done and may we be advocates of new and better ways of living that are sustainable and life-giving.
Lord in your mercy, **hear our prayer.**

May your people gathered here be ever mindful of the love of Christ and inspired by his example to embrace his way and be your agents of love in a hurting world.
Lord in your mercy, **hear our prayer.**

May all who know sickness and pain know your healing presence in their lives and be made whole and at peace.
Lord in your mercy, **hear our prayer.**

May the dead be remade through your eternal love and rise again in your new age.
Lord in your mercy, **hear our prayer.**

Through Christ you have gifted us with all we need for the abundant life you have offered. Remember your love for us and lead us ever deeper into relationship with you and with one another, through Christ we pray, who with you and the Holy Spirit are One God, eternal and almighty. **Amen.**

EASTER *Early or Vigil Service*

Alleluia Christ is Risen! Hear our prayers offered this night from hearts gladdened by the hope of eternal life as we say, Lord in your mercy, hear our prayer.

Grant your church to always hold fast to the example of Christ's life and the hope of His resurrection.
Lord in your mercy, **hear our prayer.**

Fill the hearts of this nation with hope, peace, and a willingness to work together to build a nation where everyone has the opportunity to thrive and to live into their potential.
Lord in your mercy, **hear our prayer.**

Inhabit the lives of all gathered here, be light that dispels all darkness, vanquishing our fears and giving us the courage to love boldly.
Lord in your mercy, **hear our prayer.**

Fill our hearts with gratitude and thankfulness for the marvelous and abundant diversity of life and empower us to be stewards of your creation that all future generations may glory in all that you have created for us.
Lord in your mercy, **hear our prayer.**

Bring wholeness and healing to all who suffer in body, mind, or spirit, that they might have peace and abundant life.
Lord in your mercy, **hear our prayer.**

We give thanks for the lives of those who have already entered into your glory, and we ask that we too may one day arise in your eternal kingdom.
Lord in your mercy, **hear our prayer.**

Most gracious God, in Christ your love was made manifest in our world. Embolden us to courageously continue his ministry and to face without fear where love might take us confident in Christ's promise to stand with us and walk with us always. **Amen.**

EASTER *Principal Service*

Gracious God whose love defeated even death, hear and answer our deepest hopes and needs as you did for the women who discovered the empty tomb and hear our prayers as we say, Lord in your mercy, **hear our prayer.**

Your church is the Body of Christ, constituted and empowered to continue to proclaim Christ's resurrection, strengthen and embolden us to be persistent in our proclamation.
Lord in your mercy, **hear our prayer.**

Our world still falls short of the full blossoming of human potential. Open the eyes and hearts of the world's leaders to pursue peace and human thriving for all people.
Lord in your mercy, **hear our prayer.**

Help us to see the risen Christ in the world around. Guide us into the work you have given us to do so that the ministries of Jesus might continue, that the world might know his healing and love through our actions.
Lord in your mercy, **hear our prayer.**

You have placed us in a glorious creation and charged us with its care. Grant us wisdom and a willingness to protect our environment so that future generations might now the fullness of its beauty and abundance.
Lord in your mercy, **hear our prayer.**

Bring healing and wholeness to our lives and to all who suffer in any way. Grant that they might feel Christ's caring touch on their hurts. [Especially we pray for...*prayer list.]*
Lord in your mercy, **hear our prayer.**

Christ's resurrection opened for us the way to eternal life. Grant that we all may continue on Christ's pathway and enter into your eternal reign and rise again with all the saints who have gone before.
Lord in your mercy, **hear our prayer.**

Glorious Lord, you have promised to be with us always fulfill now your promises for us and grant our prayers as may be best of us and always in accord with your will. All this we ask through our advocate and redeemer, Christ Jesus who lives with you and the Holy Spirit, eternally one God. **Amen.**

MONDAY IN EASTER WEEK

With gladness of hearts, we make haste to offer you our prayers, Risen Lord, saying, Lord in your mercy hear our prayer.

Like our sister Mary of Magdala, we too long to see you, Christ. Open your disciples in this age to the reality of your presence among us and send us anew into the joyful task of shouting out good news.
Lord in your mercy, **hear our prayer.**

May our government and all its leaders embody your care for justice and mercy. May our leaders in towns and counties and cities and capitals rejoice in serving others and may the world stage see an end to the evil of war and a reorientation toward a global goal of peace.
Lord in your mercy, **hear our prayer.**

Open our eyes to see the needs in our own neighborhoods and parishes. Use us to answer prayers and to be a healing presence to those around us.
Lord in your mercy, **hear our prayer.**

Blanket this community with peace and concord. Give us an appreciation for our neighbors and a desire to know them well. Give us your love for the world around us.
Lord in your mercy, **hear our prayer.**

Bless and heal those who are anxious of heart, hopeless in spirit or ill. Give them relief from suffering and a sense of wholeness and peace.
Lord in your mercy, **hear our prayer.**

We pray for he departed with a special care for those who mourn their passing. Welcome them with light and joy into your kingdom.
Lord in your mercy, **hear our prayer.**

With joy in the promises given through Christ's resurrection, these prayers are offered in a spirit of love to you Eternal God, giving thanks to you, your Son, our savior, and the Holy Spirit. **Amen.**

TUESDAY IN EASTER WEEK

We lift up our voices in prayer and supplication, saying, Lord in your mercy, hear our prayer.

You have given to your people, the church, the gift of the Holy Spirit to lead us into greater love and greater understanding, grant us the strength to follow.
Lord in your mercy, **hear our prayer.**

Fill the hearts of this world's leaders with a desire to be servants to justice and mercy and to see the dignity of all people. Grant us the peace which passes understanding.
Lord in your mercy, **hear our prayer.**

Inspire our imaginations to find ways to undo the damage we have done to the environment and climate. Grant us the courage to make bold changes.
Lord in your mercy, **hear our prayer.**

Grow in us the joy we have experienced through Christ's resurrection and give us willing hearts and hands to continue His work in this community. Grant us resilience to continue our mission.
Lord in your mercy, **hear our prayer.**

Arouse in us the faith to see in Christ's victory an invitation to abundant life in the here and now. Grant us hearts overflowing with joyous love.
Lord in your mercy, **hear our prayer.**

Let your healing spirit descend upon all who suffer. Grant them release from their pain and fears.
Lord in your mercy, **hear our prayer.**

Welcome the dying, comfort the grieving, and bring us, at the end of our earthly journey into your loving embrace. Grant us all the fulfillment of your promises.
Lord in your mercy, **hear our prayer.**

Through Christ your power entered into the world in new and wondrous ways, enter into our lives that we may know and share your glorious love that transforms all human life. We ask this through the one who has conquered death and opened the pathway to eternal life for all people, this same Christ who with You and the Holy Spirit lives and reigns, forever. **Amen.**

WEDNESDAY IN EASTER WEEK

Risen and holy Savior, we know you in the breaking of bread and the sharing of the cup of your new covenant. As we wait in anticipation for that holy meal, we offer you the crumbs of our hearts as we say, Lord in your mercy, hear our prayer

Grant your church a spirit that allows us to take on and tackle projects that will improve our ministry, serve our neighbors and better our own spiritual lives.
Lord in your mercy, **hear our prayer.**

Grant our nation a spirit of renewal, revival, and respect for one another and for those who live in different countries and circumstances then we do.
Lord in your mercy, **hear our prayer.**

Give to people in every place those things that are necessary for life – food, shelter, clothing, friends, gratifying work, and meaningful worship of you.
Lord in your mercy, **hear our prayer.**

Grant that all those who feel isolated and alone may turn to a true follower of Jesus and find a place to worship, to grow and to be in community.
Lord in your mercy, **hear our prayer.**

Give to all those who lead or manage others in government, workplaces, homes, and churches the integrity to do what is right, joy in the work they are called to do, and wisdom to avoid temptation.
Lord in your mercy, **hear our prayer.**

Grant healing to those who are sick, suffering or in need.
Lord in your mercy, **hear our prayer.**

Give the dying a place at your heavenly banquet and grant them peace at their end.
Lord in your mercy, **hear our prayer.**

These prayers and praises are yours, Almighty Father, who together with your Son and the Holy Spirit, reign this day and always. **Amen.**

THURSDAY IN EASTER WEEK

God of peace, enter in and hear us as we lift up our hopes and needs to you as we say, Lord in your mercy, hear our prayer.

That your church may be a non-anxious presence in a world wracked by turmoil and conflict and place of peace and sanctuary for all we pray.
Lord in your mercy, **hear our prayer.**

That this nation may fulfill its promises, offer dignity to all its people, and be an advocate for justice, mercy, and peace in the world we pray.
Lord in your mercy, **hear our prayer.**

That our local community might be a place where children might grow up in peace and security with opportunities to grow into the people they were created to be we pray.
Lord in your mercy, **hear our prayer.**

That this assembly might grow in faith and work together to discern and carry out your mission for us we pray.
Lord in your mercy, **hear our prayer.**

That those impacted by sickness and injury might find relief in your healing love, be returned to wholeness, and know the peace which is beyond comprehension we pray.
Lord in your mercy, **hear our prayer.**

That the dead might be made complete in your love and that we may all rise again together in your new age we pray.
Lord in your mercy, **hear our prayer.**

In Christ you have overcome the darkness which shrouded human life and given us freedom and reason for hope. In thankfulness for your salvation, we offer these prayers through Christ, who with you and the holy Spirit stand over all creation forever. **Amen.**

FRIDAY IN EASTER WEEK

Remembering that Jesus showed love for his friends by sharing food and fellowship, let us pray for the followers of Jesus, for ourselves, and for the world as we say, Lord in your mercy, hear our prayer.

May our hearts and minds be always on you O God. Bless us with silence to hear your voice and share our thoughts with you.
Lord in your mercy, **hear our prayer.**

May our country be a place where children can thrive in their homes, in their families, their schools, and communities. Bless each young life with safety, confidence and love.
Lord in your mercy, **hear our prayer.**

May our homes be free from anger and division. Bless each of us with patience in our relationships and peace in our households.
Lord in your mercy, **hear our prayer.**

May our communities be places of welcome for those who are not of our faith, our race, our politics, or our preferences. Bless us with the knowing of strangers and angels.
Lord in your mercy, **hear our prayer.**

May our prayers for healing be heard for these friends and acquaintances, that your grace might provide them with restoration.
Lord in your mercy, **hear our prayer.**

May our loved ones depart this life in confidence, without fear. Bless our own leaving with peace and the nearness of loved ones.
Lord in your mercy, **hear our prayer.**

When we are anxious and stray from you, O God. Keep us safely in your hands and hear our prayers for the world and its people. Grant them as may be best for us. In the name of the Father, the Son, and the Holy Spirit. **Amen.**

SATURDAY IN EASTER WEEK

We have gathered to offer you praise and ask a response to our hopes and needs; hear us now as pray; Lord in your mercy, hear our prayer.

Let your church be a herald of your Good News and a visible sign of your gracious love to all the world.
Lord in your mercy, **hear our prayer.**

Let our nation be place of peace and goodwill amongst all people and a positive source of hope for all the world to see.
Lord in your mercy, **hear our prayer.**

Let us learn to be advocates for a peaceful and sustainable future that future generations may know the abundance of creation and call us blessed for our willingness to change.
Lord in your mercy, **hear our prayer.**

Let this assembly know of your presence with us and strengthen us to carry on your work of healing and reconciliation.
Lord in your mercy, **hear our prayer.**

Let all who suffer in any way know release from their pain, their worry, and their fear. Grant them wholeness and hope.
Lord in your mercy, **hear our prayer.**

Let the dying know of your love and of the welcome they will receive into your holy presence and let all of us see in death the hope won for us through the mighty passion of Christ.
Lord in your mercy, **hear our prayer.**

You have led your people through fear into promise again and again. Through Christ's resurrection give us courage to strive for the promise in our lives. All this we ask through the one who loves us and asks of us our whole selves, Jesus Christ, who with you and the Holy Spirit bestrides creation in this and all ages. **Amen.**

SECOND SUNDAY OF EASTER

Joyful in the light of your love and your invitation to abundant life in Christ, we offer to you know the prayers of our deepest longings and hopes saying, Lord in your mercy, hear our prayer.

Lord, give us hands that reach out to the poor, the imprisoned, the hungry, the homeless, the sinful, the undesirable in the spirit of your love. Help our indifference.
Lord in your mercy, **hear our prayer.**

Lord, give us voices to proclaim the good news of your justice to all the persecuted and persecutors of the world. Help our lethargy.
Lord in your mercy, **hear our prayer.**

Lord, give us leaders that work toward justice and life for all people and nations. Help our apathy.
Lord in your mercy, **hear our prayer.**

Lord, give us churches that welcome all your beloved and strive to walk your way of love. Help our desire to change.
Lord in your mercy, **hear our prayer.**

Lord, give us bodies, minds, and spirits that are hopeful and healthy. Help our sickness and our sin. [Especially we pray for...*prayer list*.]
Lord in your mercy, **hear our prayer.**

Lord, give us the promise of eternal life in you. Help us to be your signs in the world, that we might impart peace to the dying and comfort to the grieving. Help our inadequacy.
Lord in your mercy, **hear our prayer.**

Heavenly Father you desire nothing but life in abundance for us. Give us the courage to claim that life, and the conviction to proclaim your goodness in all we do. We ask this through your Son, our risen Lord, Jesus Christ. **Amen.**

THIRD SUNDAY OF EASTER

We come to you Lord as your people, raised for abundant life and as heralds of your Good News. Hear now the prayers of your people as we say, Lord in your mercy, hear our prayer.

You were present with the ancient disciples, be present to us now and lead your church, that we might more fully embrace your mission.
Lord in your mercy, **hear our prayer.**

You opened Paul's eyes to the possibilities of Christ's love and sacrifice. Open the eyes of our leaders and of all in positions of authority that they too might zealously pursue Christ's path.
Lord in your mercy, **hear our prayer.**

Strengthen our faith and encourage us in our doubts, that we might cling to you and never lose hope.
Lord in your mercy, **hear our prayer.**

We have been placed in an abundant creation. Grant us wisdom to use it sustainably and equitably so that people everywhere may share in its bounty.
Lord in your mercy, **hear our prayer.**

You healed and brought comfort to those in pain and illness. Bringing healing to our brokenness and to all who suffer in any way. [Especially for …prayer list.]
Lord in your mercy, **hear our prayer.**

You came to live and die just as we do. Fill our lives with your blessing and be with us in death that we might rise again with Christ in the new age.
Lord in your mercy, **hear our prayer.**

Loving creator and sustainer, we are your renewed people, eager to live in your life and to reflect your mercy into the world around us. Hear our prayers and respond so that we may more fully live the life you created us for. All this we ask through our Lord, Christ Jesus, who reigns with you and the Holy Spirit now and always. **Amen.**

FOURTH SUNDAY OF EASTER

When our valleys are full of shadows Lord, send us the light of your son Jesus, that we might find our way. Shepherd of our heart, comfort us with your overflowing love, hear our prayers offered with thanksgiving and sincerity as we say, Lord in your mercy hear our prayer.

When our cups seem empty Lord, fill them with your love so that our acts of service to the world overflow and benefit others.
Lord in your mercy, **hear our prayer.**

When our nation and other countries walk in darkness Lord, fill our leaders with hearts that beat for peace, justice, and provision for all people.
Lord in your mercy, **hear our prayer.**

When our bodies are ill and our minds are full of turmoil Lord, send us the peace of your presence and give us the gift of your healing.
Lord in your mercy, **hear our prayer.**

When the hungry go unfilled and the hurting are left alone Lord, melt our hearts that we might be your hands at work serving those in need.
Lord in your mercy, **hear our prayer.**

When our time on earth is ended Lord, guide us into the green pastures of your kingdom that we might live in your kingdom this day and always.
Lord in your mercy, **hear our prayer.**

Accept the prayers of your sheep O Lord and grant us peace in our day that we might live out our lives to the glory of your son Jesus Christ who reigns with you and your Holy Spirit, forever and ever. **Amen.**

FIFTH SUNDAY OF EASTER

Glorious, creating, and sustaining God; who made and cares for the world with love and mercy; hear and answer the prayers of your people as we say, Lord in your mercy, hear our prayer.

Encourage and embolden us, your people, that we might fully live into our potential and take up Christ's healing mission with courage and persistence.
Lord in your mercy, **hear our prayer.**

Open the hearts of those who hold authority in the world that they might focus their gaze and attention on policies that promote peace, wellness, and the relief of suffering.
Lord in your mercy, **hear our prayer.**

Help us to see the needs of those we encounter in our daily lives and grant us a desire for generosity that we might respond with love and mercy.
Lord in your mercy, **hear our prayer.**

Grant us wisdom and determination to respond effectively to climate change; help us reclaim our intended role as stewards, and not destroyers, of your wonderfully created world.
Lord in your mercy, **hear our prayer.**

Bring your healing presence to all who suffer in any way. Give them strength to cope and bring skilled and healing caregivers into their lives. [Especially we pray for…*prayer list.*]
Lord in your mercy, **hear our prayer.**

Be with those who are in their last days, those who watch over them, and those who will grieve their loss. Take them into your eternal care and reunite us with them in your new age.
Lord in your mercy, **hear our prayer.**

Lord, Creation sings your praise in its very being. Help us to hear the song and to add our own voices. Be present to us and guide us on the Way of your Son, our Lord, Jesus, through whom we pray and give thanks. **Amen.**

SIXTH SUNDAY OF EASTER

Holy God send your spirit to comfort, inform, direct, and guide us to your truth in this life and in the life to come. Hear and respond to us as we say, Lord in your mercy, hear our prayer.

Gift all those who love you with the will and discipline to follow your commands.
Lord in your mercy, **hear our prayer.**

Inspire those who fear that you are far from them. Guide us to be in their lives so that they may know with certainty that your love is always present.
Lord in your mercy, **hear our prayer.**

Give our national and international leaders and all who hold authority over your people strong hearts filled with compassion, mercy, and justice.
Lord in your mercy, **hear our prayer.**

Comfort those who are sick in body, mind, or spirit. Grant them an awareness of your faithful care and your deep desire for the restoration of all things. [Especially we pray for...*prayer list*].
Lord in your mercy, **hear our prayer.**

Guide us into vocations, relationships, study, and actions that delight and sustain us as we seek to follow your way of life and love.
Lord in your mercy, **hear our prayer.**

Welcome the dying who come home to dwell at last in your heavenly kingdom, comfort those who weep or mourn with the knowledge of salvation.
Lord in your mercy, **hear our prayer.**

Heavenly Father, overturn the empty doubts and fears we keep stored in the secret places of our thoughts and fill us instead with the peace that only you can give. Grant us a life lived in the joy of serving your Son, Jesus Christ, who with you and the Holy Spirit dwells in love eternal. **Amen.**

SEVENTH SUNDAY OF EASTER

God, you have never lost hope in us. Help us to live into that hope and fulfill Jesus' prayer that we may all be one in Christ. In gratitude, and anticipation of your will being made manifest in our lives, we offer our prayers as we say, **Lord in your mercy, hear our prayer.**

We pray for the people of God, across the world and for the church in all its wondrous diversity, that we might find common ground for continuing Christ's mission together, grounded in our common love of Christ.
Lord in your mercy, **hear our prayer.**

We pray for those in leadership in all the nations of the world. Guide them, inspire them, grant them wisdom so that there might be peace and shared prosperity across the whole human race.
Lord in your mercy, **hear our prayer.**

We pray for the places we call home. Embolden us to use our gifts and energies to proclaim our hope in you through service to our neighbors.
Lord in your mercy, **hear our prayer.**

We pray for the natural world that sustains us. Help us to be effective stewards of the environment and natural resources so that the created abundance of life may not be despoiled or destroyed.
Lord in your mercy, **hear our prayer.**

We pray for all who suffer in soul, body, or mind. Grant them healing and release them from pain and suffering. [Especially we offer prayer for… *prayer list*.]
Lord in your mercy, **hear our prayer.**

We pray for those who have died, that they may rest in peace and rise in glory in your promised new age.
Lord in your mercy, **hear our prayer.**

God of love and wonder, open our eyes to your presence, reassure our hearts of your promises, embolden us for mission, and hear and answer our prayers that we might more perfectly be bearers of your love. **Amen.**

PENTECOST

On this day we give thanks for the power of the Holy Spirit that moves through our lives and leads us further along the way of Christ. Hear and answer the prayers of your people as we say, Lord in your mercy, **hear our prayer.**

Grant us a spirit of reverence for your glory and bless your church that it may always follow you into the world without fear to share your Good News.
Lord in your mercy, **hear our prayer.**

Lodge the spirit of justice in our hearts and in the hearts of all who hold authority over others in this world, that we may all strive for a more perfect human society.
Lord in your mercy, **hear our prayer.**

Grant us a spirit of commitment that we might give ourselves wholly to Christ's invitation to walk his way and continue his mission of healing and reconciliation.
Lord in your mercy, hear our prayer.

Grow in us a spirit of wisdom that we might be effective stewards of your creation, ensuring the abundance and diversity of the natural world for generations to come.
Lord in your mercy, **hear our prayer.**

May the spirit of merciful generosity be ours to embolden and encourage us to respond to the needs of our neighbors and to build a community where every person has the opportunity to thrive.
Lord in your mercy, **hear our prayer.**

Send your healing spirit to all who suffer or are in distress. [Especially we pray for...*prayer list.*]
Lord in your mercy, **hear our prayer.**

And we ask that your spirit of forgiveness and love be extended to all who have died, that they and we may someday rise in your new kingdom.
Lord in your mercy, **hear our prayer.**

Glorious, loving, and creating God; you have never abandoned us and have always offered the lighted path out of our own darkness. Hear and respond to our prayers and may your Holy Spirit blow mightily in our own lives. **Amen.**

TRINITY SUNDAY

Let us lift up the intentions and hopes of our deepest selves to God as we offer our prayers, saying, Lord in your mercy, hear our prayer.

God of Wisdom, give to your people discerning minds and open hearts that they may inhabit fully the body of Christ and join together to fulfill your will.
Lord in your mercy, **hear our prayer.**

God of Justice, grant to the leaders of this nation and of all nations a love of peace and a yearning for reconciliation.
Lord in your mercy, **hear our prayer.**

God of peace, bring an end to all wars, freedom for the oppressed, food for the hungry, and safety for the endangered.
Lord in your mercy, **hear our prayer.**

God of love, open us to perceive the joys and sufferings in our midst that we may celebrate with and share the tears of our neighbors.
Lord in your mercy, **hear our prayer.**

God almighty, give strength to those who fear, stand with those who are alone, bring healing to those who are afflicted, and hope to those who are hopeless.
Lord in your mercy, **hear our prayer.**

God eternal, hold in your care all those who have died and grant that they and we may one day rise on the day of new Creation.
Lord in your mercy, **hear our prayer.**

Loving Relationship is the very being of God, and you have made us in your image so that through relationship with you, and one another, we might know abundant life. We ask these prayers now in the name of the Son who with the Father and Holy Spirit reigns over heaven and earth and across all ages, forever. **Amen.**

LECTIONARY YEAR C

PROPER 1: *Sunday closest to May 11*

Let us pray for our church, our families, ourselves and the world saying, Lord in your mercy, hear our prayer.

We love this church and ask for growth in membership, in joy and in spirituality. Give us hope.
Lord in your mercy, **hear our prayer.**

We love our country and ask for growth in compassion and cooperation. Give us kindness.
Lord in your mercy, **hear our prayer.**

We love our neighbors and ask for their wellbeing and safety. Give us peace.
Lord in your mercy, **hear our prayer.**

We love your creation and the many plants and animals that you have given to our care. We ask for their protection. Give us solutions.
Lord in your mercy, **hear our prayer.**

We love our sick and suffering neighbors. We ask for their healing, give them your grace. [For…*prayer list*].
Lord in your mercy, **hear our prayer.**

We love our relationship with you as Father and we ask for deeper affection for our siblings around the world. Give us compassion.
Lord in your mercy, **hear our prayer**

We love those who we long to see again, and we ask for their life eternal to be lived in love. Give us comfort.
Lord in your mercy, **hear our prayer.**

We offer these prayers O Lord, in the name of your Son who lives and reigns with you and the Holy Spirit, one God forever and ever. **Amen.**

PROPER 2: *Sunday closest to May 18*

Loving God, we have come together to offer you praise, to know your presence and to lift the needs of our hearts and souls to you as we pray, Lord in your mercy, hear our prayer.

For the church of Christ in all its diversity. Guide us into ways of working as one for the spread of your kingdom.
Lord in your mercy, **hear our prayer.**

For this nation and for all nations and their leaders, that the people of the world might recognize that what they share in common is much more than the ways they differ, so that they might work for the peace and well-being of humanity.
Lord in your mercy, **hear our prayer.**

For this congregation, so that we might forge closer bonds with one another and work together to show heaven's light on our neighbors.
Lord in your mercy, **hear our prayer.**

For the natural world and for our use of its resources, reconcile our needs with its capacity and show us how to live abundantly and sustainably.
Lord in your mercy, **hear our prayer.**

For all who are beset by illness, injury, or impairment and for all who care for them, might they know your presence and feel your healing power in their lives. [Especially we lift up …prayer list.]
Lord in your mercy, **hear our prayer.**

For those who have died and for those at the threshold of death, that your will for them might be complete and that they may reside in the glory of your eternal presence and love.
Lord in your mercy, **hear our prayer.**

Show us O Lord how we might bear the good fruit of your love and fulfill your dreams for us that your glory might dispel our fears and propel our hopes. All this we ask through the One who brings peace and reconciliation, Jesus Christ. **Amen.**

LECTIONARY YEAR C

PROPER 3: *Sunday closest to May 25*

Let us turn to the Lord who inclines his ear to us; offering God our prayers, petitions, and thanksgivings as we say, Lord in your mercy, hear our prayer.

May the church be a place of welcome and sanctuary for all who worship. May the church universal be a light and blessing to all people and nations.
Lord in your mercy, **hear our prayer.**

May all who have authority and leadership in this nation, this state, and this community be servants to the common good. May they find joy in their vocation and be compassionate and wise leaders for the good of all.
Lord in your mercy, **hear our prayer.**

May this community be a place of prosperity and peace for all who live here. May we have adequate resources for all and serve the needs of those who do not have what is necessary in life.
Lord in your mercy, **hear our prayer.**

May those who face war and danger and persecution in the world find safety and peace. May we keep those who face injustice and violence in our prayers and seek ways to serve them ourselves.
Lord in your mercy, **hear our prayer.**

May healing and grace rain down on all who seek cure and comfort from disease and injury. [Lord, give your healing to those we offer to you now… *prayer list.*]
Lord in your mercy, **hear our prayer.**

May the dying leave this life in peace and hope. May those who mourn be comforted with your love and our presence.
Lord in your mercy, **hear our prayer.**

May these prayers find favor with you this day, Lord God. May we leave this day nourished by your presence and ready to serve you with our voices, actions, and lives. **Amen.**

PROPER 4: *Sunday closest to June 1*

O Lord of unknowable power and wisdom, hear the pleas of your people and fulfill their needs and hopes as may best for us as we say, Lord in your mercy, hear our prayer.

We pray for that holy mystery, the church, that it proclaims its message of transformation with joy and humility so that all people might know the abundant life of Christ.
Lord in your mercy, **hear our prayer.**

We pray for the nations of the world, that conflicts might cease and that enemies might be reconciled so that peace might reign across the globe.
Lord in your mercy, **hear our prayer.**

We pray for this assembly, that we might hear and respond to God's word and presence and be renewed and reenergized for the work of ministry to which we have been called.
Lord in your mercy, **hear our prayer.**

We pray for the whole earth, for the preservation of the oceans, forests, and creatures which sustain the richness of life and that we should remember our divine role as stewards of this wondrous creation.
Lord in your mercy, **hear our prayer.**

We pray for those who are sick and injured, and for those whose lives have been diminished that they may know your healing presence and find wholeness and peace of mind. [Especially we pray for...*prayer list*.]
Lord in your mercy, **hear our prayer.**

We pray for all who have died, that they might be welcomed into the divine presence and be raised up anew in your coming kingdom.
Lord in your mercy, **hear our prayer.**

Lord God, your steadfast love has preserved your people across time; be with us today and show us the path to eternal and abundant life; through our Lord and Savior, Jesus Christ, who with you and the Holy Spirit reigns eternal. **Amen.**

PROPER 5: *Sunday closest to June 8*

Let us call out to our God and ask his blessings, call out to God with the true content of our hearts as we say, Lord in your mercy, hear our prayer.

For the church around the world that it will call out to those who seek the love of God and be places of hope for those who enter into worship and discipleship.
Lord in your mercy, **hear our prayer.**

For each person here today that we will be the hands and feet of Jesus in the world.
Lord in your mercy, **hear our prayer.**

For the needs of our nation, to feed the hungry, to house the homeless, to provide for those in great need, and to shelter and protect the vulnerable.
Lord in your mercy, **hear our prayer.**

For the people of the world that live in fear and poverty. For solutions to war, violence, persecution, and injustice so that all may have what is necessary for life and none are left bereft of basic needs.
Lord in your mercy, **hear our prayer.**

For those who are awaiting diagnosis and who are involved in treatment; for those who live with chronic pain and illness; for the addicted and tormented; for the unstable and uncertain that healing of body, mind and spirit will prevail.
Lord in your mercy, **hear our prayer.**

For the sick and those in need of comfort. [Especially for...*prayer list.*]
Lord in your mercy, **hear our prayer.**

For those near death and for those who have died, that all may abide with you in your heavenly kingdom.
Lord in your mercy, **hear our prayer.**

For the kingdom, the power and the glory are yours our Holy God: Father, Son and Holy Spirit. **Amen.**

PROPER 6: *Sunday closest to June 15*

Forgiving God, answer our prayers through the power of Christ, whose atoning love has made possible our redemption. Hear us as we say,
Lord in your mercy, hear our prayer.

Shower your blessings on the people of God throughout the world, strengthen their faith and grant them the wisdom and encourage to share your good news with joy and serve the world with love.
Lord in your mercy, **hear our prayer.**

Bless our nation and raise up leaders devoted to justice, liberty, and peace who will pursue policies meant to create opportunities for human thriving for all people.
Lord in your mercy, **hear our prayer.**

Strengthen this assembly and lead us forward in mission and ministry for the building of the kingdom in this community.
Lord in your mercy, **hear our prayer.**

Embolden us to face with courage and hope the environmental challenges which threaten your good creation. Let us be advocates for a sustainable and prosperous future.
Lord in your mercy, **hear our prayer.**

Heal the sick, mend the injured, bring peace to the anxious, and grant to all who suffer release from their pain and an understanding of the peace which passes all understanding.
Lord in your mercy, **hear our prayer.**

Welcome the dying, that your will for them might be fulfilled, and grant them and us an entrance into the glorious kingdom of light at the end of this age.
Lord in your mercy, **hear our prayer.**

Let your peace settle upon us and remain with us, and let our prayers so move our hearts that we might take up the call to be agents of your love in all that we do and with all whom we meet. We ask thin in the name of Christ, our Lord. **Amen.**

PROPER 7: *Sunday closest to June 22*

God there are no places your love cannot penetrate; give us eyes to see you in darkness, ears to hear you in silence, and minds that rest in your stillness. Hear these prayers and the prayers of our deepest hearts as we say, Lord in your mercy, hear our prayer.

Grant to those who love you, and those who long to love you more, the deep desire to do your will and seek you in all times and circumstances.
Lord in your mercy, hear our prayer.

Inspire our hearts to carry your message to all those who long for your good news and send us to be your hands at work in this world and in the world to come.
Lord in your mercy, hear our prayer.

Give to those who have authority over us the desire to serve your people with mercy and justice.
Lord in your mercy, hear our prayer.

Bless us with a great unease in the face of hunger, poverty, injustice, and persecution that we might find peace only in the way of Love as demonstrated by your son Jesus, our Lord.
Lord in your mercy, hear our prayer.

Comfort the afflicted, the wounded, the sick and the dying with the certain promise of your constant love in this life and the next. [Especially we pray for...*prayer list*.]
Lord in your mercy, hear our prayer.

Welcome the dying and comfort the grieving; let their entrance into the land of light and life give us comfort and hope for our future.
Lord in your mercy, hear our prayer.

Glory and honor to you O Lord, for you are the one who seeks us out, provides for our needs, and directs our path. Bless us and keep us this day and always through the grace of your Son and the power of your Holy Spirit. **Amen.**

PROPER 8: *Sunday closest to June 29*

We turn our faces to you in expectation and confidence that you will hear us when we pray, saying, Lord in your mercy, hear our prayer.

We ask your prayers for the church universal; for true revival to bring us new ways to reach those who are wary of faith and to embrace those who find their way to us.
Lord in your mercy, **hear our prayer.**

We ask your prayers for those who lead this nation and all nations, for those who lead in towns and communities around the world that compassion and service will overcome fear and hatred and that we might have peace and relationships among all people.
Lord in your mercy, **hear our prayer.**

We ask your prayers for this assembly, that we might experience the living Christ and know, in our deepest selves, that we are loved and were created with purpose.
Lord in your mercy, **hear our prayer.**

We ask you prayers for the natural world and all who labor to preserve and protect it for all future generations.
Lord in your mercy, **hear our prayer.**

We ask your prayers for those who need healing of heart, healing of mind, and healing of body. [Bless those we offer to you now...*prayer list*.]
Lord in your mercy, **hear our prayer.**

We ask your prayers for those who die alone and afraid; for those who die unexpectedly and tragically; for those who die surrounded by their families and full of faith. Bring all those beloved into your light perpetual.
Lord in your mercy, **hear our prayer.**

We offer all these prayers through Jesus Christ our Lord, our comforter, guide, and mediator. **Amen.**

PROPER 9: *Sunday closest to July 6*

God of joyous love, hear our prayers and be swift to answer us as we say, Lord in your mercy, hear our prayer.

Embolden your church. Let it be ever in the world seeking to bring the healing power of the living Christ to a wounded world.
Lord in your mercy, **hear our prayer.**

Hold our nation in your care, grant courage to those who stand for the equality of all persons and who advocate justice for all, and guide us in becoming a more perfect reflection of our founding promises.
Lord in your mercy, **hear our prayer.**

Strengthen the faith of those gathered here today and grant us to see the fruits of our ministry that we might be encouraged in the work you have called us to.
Lord in your mercy, **hear our prayer.**

We offer thanksgiving for the rich bounty of your creation. Guide us in working to ensure its abundance is shared equitably and sustainably.
Lord in your mercy, **hear our prayer.**

Relieve the suffering of those impacted by illness, injury, and impairment, and grant them a share in the peace which passes understanding.
[Especially we lift up…*prayer list.*]
Lord in your mercy, **hear our prayer.**

Embrace the dying in your eternal love, shroud them with your grace, and grant them entrance into the place of light and life at your side.
Lord in your mercy, **hear our prayer.**

Throughout history, you have empowered your people to make your love manifest in the lives of those who have known suffering. Empower us to today to be agents of your love and heralds of your gospel to a world in need of both; and all this we ask through our Lord, Jesus who is your Christ and who reigns with you and the Holy Spirit eternally. **Amen.**

PROPER 10: *Sunday closest to July 13*

The creator of all that is has called us into relationship; let us now offer our prayers to the one whose love and compassion are the source of all life, saying, Lord in your mercy, hear our prayer.

Shower your blessings on your church throughout the world. Help us to be neighbors to all people; strangers and friends, those close by and those far away, of every land and language and culture.
Lord in your mercy, **hear our prayer.**

Guide the leaders of our nation and of all nations to extend the hand of friendship, that we might work together for a more peaceful world.
Lord in your mercy, **hear our prayer.**

Inspire and embolden us that we might show neighborly love to one another to build a better tomorrow.
Lord in your mercy, **hear our prayer.**

Let us glory in your abundant creation and commit ourselves to its care and sustenance.
Lord in your mercy, **hear our prayer.**

Remind us to make time for those who suffer or who are isolated, that we might magnify your love in our lives. [Especially for those who have sought our prayers, for…*prayer list*.]
Lord in your mercy, **hear our prayer.**

We hold fast to your promises, especially your care for those whose earthly journey has ended. Grant that we too may come to rest in your care and rise in glory in your new age.
Lord in your mercy, **hear our prayer.**

Lord God, you formed us in love; you command us to live in your love. Hear the prayers we make in the name of the Son you sent to dwell among us, the neighbor who is attentive to all our needs, Jesus Christ our Lord. **Amen.**

PROPER 11: *Sunday closest to July 20*

Let us pray to the Most High God saying, Lord in your mercy, hear our prayer.

Grant your church such love for you that others are led into relationship with you by our faith and actions.
Lord in your mercy, **hear our prayer.**

Open the hearts of each person here to feel your presence and do your will this day and always.
Lord in your mercy, **hear our prayer.**

Bless this nation, state, and local community. Bless all nations and people. Give us leaders who seek to serve all people with justice, compassion, and care.
Lord in your mercy, **hear our prayer.**

Restore all things in your creation and heal the wounds we have inflicted on your earth and creatures.
Lord in your mercy, **hear our prayer.**

End the cycle of violence and poverty through your grace and our efforts on behalf of victims and the vulnerable.
Lord in your mercy, **hear our prayer.**

Heal all those who are sick in body, mind, or spirit. Bless us with good care through doctors, nurses, staff, medicines, and prayer. [We pray especially for...*prayer list.*]
Lord in your mercy, **hear our prayer.**

Surround the dying with your love and give strength to those who mourn. Bring all souls into the light of your perpetual love.
Lord in your mercy, **hear our prayer.**

All these we ask in the name of your son, our savior Jesus Christ, who lives and reigns with you and the holy spirit now and forever. **Amen.**

PROPER 12: *Sunday closest to July 27*

God of mercy whose care and compassion for us is beyond imagining. Hear us as you heard Abraham and answer our prayers as may be best for us and always to your glory as we say, Lord in your mercy, hear our prayer.

Guide your church that it might be a bold and fearless champion of the dignity of all people and a place of welcome and respite for the weary, the *oppressed*, and the marginalized.
Lord in your mercy, **hear our prayer.**

Open the eyes and hearts of all in authority. Grant them wisdom and compassion in the exercise of their responsibilities that they might always pursue the path of greatest good.
Lord in your mercy, **hear our prayer.**

Allow us to see the good in our neighbors that we might be forceful advocates for human thriving in all the places we call home.
Lord in your mercy, **hear our prayer.**

Remind us of our call to be the caretakers of creation and embolden us to demand urgent action to ensure environmental sustainability.
Lord in your mercy, **hear our prayer.**

Bring your healing presence into the lives of all who suffer from any distress. [Especially we lift up our prayers for...*prayer list*.]
Lord in your mercy, **hear our prayer.**

Hold the dead in your loving care and grant us also to enter into your eternal love on the day of our death.
Lord in your mercy, **hear our prayer.**

Creating and sustaining Lord, you know before we ask the longings of our hearts. Look upon us with compassion and lead us ever deeper into relationship with you so that we might more fully be the people you created us to be. All these we ask in the name of our Lord and savior, Jesus Christ. **Amen.**

PROPER 13: *Sunday closest to August 3*

Merciful God, align the desires of our hearts with your will for us and answer our prayers as may be best for us as we say, Lord in your mercy, hear our prayer.

Your holy church is a sacrament, making visible your grace and mercy. Keep it on the narrow path that leads to salvation and let it be a beacon of hope and an advocate for merciful justice throughout the world.
Lord in your mercy, **hear our prayer.**

Guide the people and leaders of our nation to see the dignity of all persons, and to work together to ensure that all persons have the opportunity to live into the potential with which they were created by you.
Lord in your mercy, **hear our prayer.**

Grant that this community of faith might be a place where your presence is known and where each of us can fully bring our gifts to bear for the building of the kingdom.
Lord in your mercy, **hear our prayer.**

Remind us of the glory of your creation and spur us into action on its behalf that the wonder of the natural world might be preserved and sustained, not only for ourselves but for all future generations.
Lord in your mercy, **hear our prayer.**

Come swiftly to the aid of all who suffer or are oppressed, for all who are ill, injured, or facing disability. Help them know peace and wholeness. [Especially we pray for…*prayer list.*]
Lord in your mercy, **hear our prayer.**

Give strength to those who stand at the threshold of mortal death and those who love and care for them. Grant them a share in your peace and reunite them in the light of your eternal kingdom.
Lord in your mercy, **hear our prayer.**

Hear these prayers which we offer with confident faith in your love and mercy and answer us that your glory may be known; through Christ our Lord and Redeemer who stands with you and the Holy Spirit, overseeing all creation now and always. **Amen.**

PROPER 14: *Sunday closest to August 10*

O God your Word comes to us, and our hearts are uplifted. Listen now, we beseech you, to the needs and thanksgivings of your people as we say, Lord in your mercy, hear our prayer.

Fill your church with faith, that our hope might embolden us to be your agents of love in all the corners of our lives.
Lord in your mercy, **hear our prayer.**

Grant wisdom, compassion, and a love of justice to the leaders of our nation that they might work for the good of all.
Lord in your mercy, **hear our prayer.**

Open our eyes to the possibilities of tomorrow; lead us to focus not just on problems but to search for solutions that we might build a sustainable way of life that honors your abundant creation.
Lord in your mercy, **hear our prayer.**

We are committed to being your people in this community at this time. Grant us discerning hearts and burning desire to share your Good News that our community might be a place where all people may thrive.
Lord in your mercy, **hear our prayer.**

Let your healing love be present in the lives of all who suffer. [Especially we pray for…*prayer list.*]
Lord in your mercy, **hear our prayer.**

Welcome the dead into your loving embrace, tend to the souls of those who grieve, and let us hold close the love of those whom we wait to see in your new age.
Lord in your mercy, **hear our prayer.**

O Generous God, you desire that we should live in love and not fear; hear our prayers, be known in our lives, and respond to the needs and hopes of your people; all this we ask through Jesus, our Lord and Savior who with you and Holy spirit lives and reigns, now and always. **Amen.**

PROPER 15: *Sunday closest to August 17*

Lord God, you have promised to be near, be with us now and hear and answer our prayers as we say, Lord in your mercy, hear our prayer.

Lead your church, that we might stand in the light of your glory in all that we do.
Lord in your mercy, **hear our prayer.**

Open the hearts and minds of those with authority in our lives and fill them with wisdom and mercy, that they might always strive only for the greatest good.
Lord in your mercy, **hear our prayer.**

Guide us and put us to work as laborers for your kingdom, that the world might see your glory and live as the people you created them to be.
Lord in your mercy, **hear our prayer.**

Give us courageous and willing hearts to be effective stewards of your Creation, that we might learn to use it sustainably.
Lord in your mercy, **hear our prayer.**

Push away fear and pain in the lives of those who suffer and bring your healing presence to them. [Especially we pray for…*prayer list.*]
Lord in your mercy, **hear our prayer.**

Enfold the dying in your love, give strength to those who mourn, and comfort those who grieve.
Lord in your mercy, **hear our prayer.**

Heavenly Father, you have shown us your love again and again, cover us with your blessings and mercy as we move through our lives, that we might reflect your love into the world. All this we ask through Christ, our Lord who with you and the Holy Spirit, lives reigns, now and always. **Amen.**

PROPER 16: *Sunday closest to August 24*

Healing God, as we gather to express the longings of our hearts, shower on us your mercy and grace as we say, Lord in your mercy, hear our prayer.

Holy Lord, shake your church, tumble us out into the world to continue the ministry of Jesus to bring wholeness to a broken world.
Lord in your mercy, **hear our prayer.**

Move the hearts of this nation and its leaders that we and they might see clearly both what holds us together and what pulls us apart, that joining together we might build a just and merciful society.
Lord in your mercy, **hear our prayer.**

Open our ears, our eyes, and our hearts to hear your call and empower our hands and feet to move closer to you through our service to others.
Lord in your mercy, **hear our prayer.**

Fill us with awe in contemplation of the glory of your Creation and shake us out of our complacency that we might be effective stewards and champions of our natural world.
Lord in your mercy, **hear our prayer.**

Tend those who suffer, bring to wholeness what is broken, reconciliation to what has been separated, and lift up what has been pressed down.
[Especially we ask your healing power for…*prayer list.*]
Lord in your mercy, **hear our prayer.**

Fulfill your promises to the dying, care for the grieving, and grant us all an entrance into your eternal loving presence.
Lord in your mercy, **hear our prayer.**

You have allowed no barriers to your loving action, hear, and fulfill our longings as may be best for us, and grant us your salvation. All these we ask in the name of Jesus, our Lord, who abides with you and the Holy Spirit forever. **Amen.**

LECTIONARY YEAR C

PROPER 17: *Sunday closest to August 31*

O Lord our God, grant that we might see the majesty of your glory in our lives and
hear our prayers as we say. Lord in your mercy, hear our prayer.

Lead your church into humility and may her leaders be first her servants, seeking only and always to glorify you in their lives.
Lord in your mercy, **hear our prayer.**

Give us selfless civil leaders who are zealous for truth, justice, and mercy and whose efforts build up the whole community and bring people together.
Lord in your mercy, **hear our prayer.**

Embolden us to make the difficult choices to ensure the continued abundance of your Creation.
Lord in your mercy, **hear our prayer.**

Make us good neighbors and open our eyes to see you in the eyes of those we encounter, that together we might build a community where everyone can thrive and live into their potential.
Lord in your mercy, **hear our prayer.**

Give peace and strength to those who are sick or injured or who endure suffering in all its myriad forms. [Especially we lift up...*prayer list.*]
Lord in your mercy, **hear our prayer.**

Grant the dead entrance into your eternal embrace and grant us also to enter and join them there when we leave this world.
Lord in your mercy, **hear our prayer.**

God of Glory, through your Son, you have showed us the strength of your love, grant that we might follow in His path and continue his ministry until His return; through the same Son, our Lord, who with you and the Holy Spirit lives and reigns, one God, forever. **Amen.**

PROPER 18: *Sunday closest to September 7*

Most loving and glorious God, hear us we implore you and act speedily to answer our prayers as we say, Lord in your mercy, hear our prayer.

You have blessed your church across time with leaders of true faith, grant your church today wisdom and discernment that we might effectively share the good news of Jesus.
Lord in your mercy, **hear our prayer.**

Give us wisdom to choose leaders of integrity, and also the courage and resolve to hold them accountable to their responsibility to build a nation where all people might thrive and know their dignity as God's created children.
Lord in your mercy, **hear our prayer.**

All our truest needs are provided by you. Open our minds and hearts to see the abundance of your creation and to boldly embrace policies that ensure no basic human needs go unmet.
Lord in your mercy, **hear our prayer.**

Fill our hearts with the love of one another as brothers and sisters in Christ and to see and be inspired by the Christ which dwells in each of us, so that together we might boldly be Christ's loving body in a hurting world.
Lord in your mercy, **hear our prayer.**

We ask healing for all who suffer, and we ask that we might be people of healing and reconciliation to those in need in our lives. [Especially we pray for...*prayer list*.]
Lord in your mercy, **hear our prayer.**

We are surrounded by the great cloud of witnesses who have been the lights of the world in their time. Grant us to follow in their example and welcome us into your eternal loving presence when it is our time to leave this earth.
Lord in your mercy, **hear our prayer.**

Most gracious Father, from the beginning you have sought to lead us into the joy possible to us through life in You. Aid us and be present with us that we might walk in the path of Jesus and live into his example. All these we offer through Christ, our Lord and highest allegiance, who with You and the Holy Spirit lives and reign always and forever. **Amen.**

LECTIONARY YEAR C

PROPER 19: *Sunday closest to September 14*

Patient and Gracious Lord, enter our hearts and move our desires to your glory as we say, Lord in your mercy, hear our prayer.

May your church always be a place of refuge and renewal, a place for the healing of lost and wounded souls.
Lord in your mercy, **hear our prayer.**

Remind us that Christian freedom is freedom from fear, from anxiety, from hate and embolden us in our civic lives that we might build a nation of peace, justice, and mercy.
Lord in your mercy, **hear our prayer.**

You created us so that we might be your partners in sustaining the abundance of creation. Grant us wisdom and a sense of urgency in addressing our environmental and climate challenges.
Lord in your mercy, **hear our prayer.**

Strengthen our parish, embolden us to share your glory in every part of our lives that the Good News of Christ might be known to all who know us.
Lord in your mercy, **hear our prayer.**

Bring healing and strength to all who suffer and let us be healers and comforters to those in need. [Especially we pray for…*prayer list.*]
Lord in your mercy, **hear our prayer.**

Embrace the dying, usher them into your eternal care and grant us an entrance into your light and love at our last day.
Lord in your mercy, **hear our prayer**

You have worked from the beginning to urge us onto the path of abundant life, continue to show guide us on the Way and welcome us back whenever we stray. Through Christ our Lord who with you and the Holy Spirit live and reign, forever and always. **Amen.**

PROPER 20: *Sunday closest to September 21*

God of Justice, let your mercy flow over us that we might experience your grace as we lift our prayers to you as we say, Lord in your mercy, hear our prayer.

That your church might be known for its love and generosity, we pray.
Lord in your mercy, **hear our prayer.**

That our nation may know peace and justice, we pray.
Lord in your mercy, **hear our prayer.**

That the environment and climate that sustains us may be protected and restored, we pray.
Lord in your mercy, **hear our prayer.**

That our parish might be a refuge for weary souls, and a place to reenergize our faith and compel our participation in Christ's mission, we pray.
Lord in your mercy, **hear our prayer.**

That all who suffer might know your healing love we pray. [Especially for…*prayer list.*]
Lord in your mercy, **hear our prayer.**

That the dead might experience your light and love for all eternity and that we may someday join them in your embrace, we pray.
Lord in your mercy, **hear our prayer.**

Almighty God, your way is the way of justice and mercy, of peace and reconciliation, of hope and generosity; hear and respond to the longings of our hearts offered in our prayers this day through the merits and love of your Son, our Lord, Jesus Christ, who with you and Holy Spirit lives and reigns. **Amen.**

LECTIONARY YEAR C

PROPER 21: *Sunday Closest to September 28*

O righteous Lord, guide us onto the pathway of glory and hear our prayers as we say, Lord in your mercy, hear our prayer.

Empower your church to fearlessly proclaim the gospel that the whole world might hear and experience your Good News.
Lord in your mercy, **hear our prayer.**

Enter the hearts and minds of our civic and cultural leaders, that their priorities are aligned with the needs and hopes of all people.
Lord in your mercy, **hear our prayer.**

Be present in our parish and in all the places we call home through our witness, that your glory might open eyes and hearts to your transforming love.
Lord in your mercy, **hear our prayer.**

Strengthen our resolve and resilience for the making of hard choices to preserve your abundant creation for all future generations.
Lord in your mercy, **hear our prayer.**

Bring the light and strength of your healing power into the darkness of all who suffer in body, mind, or spirit. [Especially we lift up those who have sought our prayers: *prayer list*].
Lord in your mercy, **hear our prayer.**

Welcome the dying, comfort the grieving, strengthen the bereft, and bring us all together again in the glory of your new age.
Lord in your mercy, **hear our prayer.**

Loving God, you have brought your word which gives life into our midst again and again; help us be faithful recipients of your grace and bearers of your good news to all whom we encounter. All we ask, we ask in the name of Jesus, our Lord and Redeemer. **Amen.**

PROPER 22: *Sunday Closest to October 5*

Almighty God, increase our faith and hear our prayers as we say, Lord in your mercy, hear our prayer.

Help you church to perceive and answer your call to serve and to build the kingdom of God.
Lord in your mercy, **hear our prayer.**

Guide the people and leaders of this nation towards unity of purpose and mutual regard, that we might be a civil society that offers hope and opportunity to all its members.
Lord in your mercy, **hear our prayer.**

Embolden us to be committed stewards of the creation you have entrusted to our care that all future generations might know its abundance.
Lord in your mercy, **hear our prayer.**

Inspire our parish to go forth and share the good news with our neighbors so that through our actions they might see a glimpse of your glorious Good News.
Lord in your mercy, **hear our prayer.**

Make your healing presence known in the lives of all who suffer and let us be instruments of your healing love. [Especially we pray for...*prayer list.*]
Lord in your mercy, **hear our prayer.**

May the dead know the brightness of your love, and may we also come to join them in your presence.
Lord in your mercy, **hear our prayer.**

God of power and might, in the life of your Son you have shown us the model and potential of our own lives. Grant us the faith to continue His mission and ministry and answer our prayers as may be best for us and to your glory, through the same Son, our Lord, Christ Jesus who with you and Holy Spirit, lives and reigns, One God, now and forever. **Amen.**

PROPER 23: *Sunday Closest to October 12*

Healing God, we praise you and we thank you for all your gifts; hear now our prayers as we lift our voices and say, Lord in your mercy, hear our prayer.

Grant that your church might be a light in the darkness, a refuge in uncertainty, and an example of love in action to bring forth a world healed by love.
Lord in your mercy, **hear our prayer.**

Bring together the people of this nation in reconciliation and peace, that together we might build a community whose foundation is the recognition of the dignity of all people.
Lord in your mercy, **hear our prayer.**

Light a fire in our hearts, that we might feel compelled to show your love in our actions and words throughout the moments of our daily lives.
Lord in your mercy, **hear our prayer.**

May your peace and justice prevail in areas of conflict around the world, that all people everywhere may know liberty and be free to live into their God-granted potential.
Lord in your mercy, **hear our prayer.**

Mend what is broken and make whole what is missing in the lives of all who suffer and grant your healing power to those in need. [Especially we pray for…*prayer list.*]
Lord in your mercy, **hear our prayer.**

May those who have died know the eternal embrace of your love and welcome each of us in the moment of our deaths into your presence.
Lord in your mercy, **hear our prayer.**

Loving God, you have always provided all that we need and showed us the path to abundant life made manifest in your Son, Our Lord, Christ Jesus, who with you and the Holy Spirit, lives and reigns, One God, now and always, **Amen.**

PROPER 24: *Sunday Closest to October 19*

God of Justice, hear us and respond as we lift our prayers to you saying, Lord in your mercy, hear our prayer.

Be with your church and guide us so that our prayers may be the seeds of ministry.
Lord in your mercy, **hear our prayer.**

Inspire our nation and its leaders, help us to rise above our divisions and work together for the common good.
Lord in your mercy, **hear our prayer.**

Be with those facing perils from natural disaster and climate change, show us how to respond effectively, and lead us to be advocates for the preservation of your creation.
Lord in your mercy, **hear our prayer.**

Be present to us in our parish, strengthen us, renew us, and embolden us, that we might eagerly share your good news in our daily lives.
Lord in your mercy, **hear our prayer.**

Heal the sick, mend the injured, renew the worn down, and lift up the oppressed. [Especially we ask your healing presence for… *prayer list*.]
Lord in your mercy, **hear our prayer.**

Welcome the dying into the comfort of your embrace, comfort those who grieve, and allow us entry into the realms of your glory when our journey through this life ends.
Lord in your mercy, **hear our prayer.**

God of Love who has never turned your back on us, be our loving and gracious God, hear and answer our prayers that we have asked through the merits of our Lord, Christ Jesus, who with You and the Holy Spirit hold all creation in your hands. **Amen.**

LECTIONARY YEAR C

PROPER 25: *Sunday Closest to October 26*

God of Justice, hear us, make your presence known to us, and respond to us as we say, Lord in your mercy, hear our prayer.

Show us how to be the body of Christ today, that your Good News might enter every human heart.
Lord in your mercy, **hear our prayer.**

Be in the eyes and ears and on the lips of our civil leaders, that they might lead through serving the welfare of all and help us to hold our leaders accountable to the needs of the whole nation.
Lord in your mercy, **hear our prayer.**

Open our hearts and our hands to our neighbor's needs, that they might encounter Christ through us.
Lord in your mercy, **hear our prayer.**

Bring peace with justice where there is conflict, bring freedom where there is oppression, and bring restoration to lands ravaged by greed, that your creation might be renewed and your purpose for us fulfilled.
Lord in your mercy, **hear our prayer.**

Be with those who suffer. Be their strength and their firm foundation throughout their struggles. [Especially we pray for…*prayer list.*]
Lord in your mercy, **hear our prayer.**

Welcome all who have died, that they might continue towards the bright future of your heavenly kingdom.
Lord in your mercy, **hear our prayer.**

Loving God, you have showed us how to love you by loving others more than we love ourselves. Hear our prayers and answer us as may be best for us and to your glory. All this we ask through Christ, our Lord, who with you and the Holy Spirit, live and reign, one God. **Amen.**

PROPER 26: *Sunday Closest to November 2*

God of Justice and Mercy, let our cries come to you that your Spirit may enter our lives, transforming us and empowering us as we say, Lord in your mercy, hear our prayer.

Lord, grant every member of your church an opportunity to welcome without reservation those curious about Jesus into the grace of your holy body, the church.
Lord in your mercy, **hear our prayer.**

We pray for our nation and for the civil order, that we may be inspired by your teachings when we discern who to elect as our leaders.
Lord in your mercy, **hear our prayer.**

Give us a deep reverence for your creation and strengthen our commitment to be faithful stewards of its abundance.
Lord in your mercy, **hear our prayer.**

Strengthen our parish and show us how to be loving neighbors so that our presence might be a steadfast symbol of hope and resilience in neighborhood.
Lord in your mercy, **hear our prayer.**

Come alongside all who suffer, give strength where there is weakness, hope where there is despair, and peace where there is turmoil. [Especially we ask your healing presence to all whom we now name, for…*prayer list.*]
Lord in your mercy, **hear our prayer.**

Grant peace to all who have died, welcoming them into your eternal presence and grant also that we may join them when our journey on this earth has ended.
Lord in your mercy, **hear our prayer.**

Your presence here is a balm to our souls. Let it also inspire us to leave from here as renewed beacons of your love that we might live in your eternal kingdom in the here and now. All this we ask through Christ, who reign with you and the Holy Spirit, One God, forever and ever. **Amen.**

PROPER 27: *Sunday Closest to November 9*

How we long to share our deepest concerns with you Lord. Hear us now as we pray, Lord in your mercy, hear our prayer.

God of love, give your universal church the will to see all people as your beloved and the mission to lift up all whom we encounter.
Lord in your mercy, **hear our prayer.**

God of new beginnings, forgive each one of us for our apathy in the light of the injustice of the world.
Lord in your mercy, **hear our prayer.**

God of mercy, grant to those who serve the needy an endless stream of volunteers, resources, and hope, that all might be provided for and that we might find a place to serve in your name.
Lord in your mercy, **hear our prayer.**

God of justice, give our leaders a sense of true vocation in service to the greater good and bless us with those who are willing to serve with compassion, wisdom, and clarity.
Lord in your mercy, **hear our prayer.**

God of hope, restore to fullness of health those who are ill, injured, or suffering from despair or anxiety. Bring peace to all who suffer. [Especially we pray for...*prayer list.*]
Lord in your mercy, **hear our prayer.**

God of our birthing, God of our dying, bless all those who depart this world in faith a place with you in your eternal kingdom.
Lord in your mercy, **hear our prayer.**

God who hears our prayers and uses us to answer the prayers of others, we ask that you answer these our heartfelt prayers in the way that best serves your purposes. Through Jesus Christ our Lord, who lives and reigns with you and the holy spirit, one God forever and ever. **Amen.**

PROPER 28: *Sunday Closest to November 16*

Holy Lord, be among us, hear us, and fulfill the hope of our prayers as we say, Lord in your mercy, hear our prayer.

Bestow your grace upon your church and lend us your strength so that we might boldly proclaim and live out the good news of Jesus Christ.
Lord in your mercy, **hear our prayer.**

Shower wisdom on those who hold authority in our lives, that they might seek to lead through service to the greatest good.
Lord in your mercy, **hear our prayer.**

Embolden us to be the body of Christ in our local community, that our presence might be a pledge of our commitment to love our neighbors.
Lord in your mercy, **hear our prayer.**

Arouse in us the desire to protect and sustain your abundant creation, that our world may remain a place of wonder and sustenance for future generations.
Lord in your mercy, **hear our prayer.**

Bring your healing power to bear in the lives of all who endure illness or injury, that that they may know peace, and arouse us to be people of care and reconciliation. [Especially we pray for...*prayer list.*]
Lord in your mercy, **hear our prayer.**

Take into your loving arms all those who have died that they might grow in love and devotion to you and bring us once again into the presence of those we have loved in your eternal kingdom.
Lord in your mercy, **hear our prayer.**

Blessed Lord, you have longed for the turning of every human heart and have showed us in word and deed the path of promise that leads to you. Hear and answer our prayers, that we might see more fully, your kingdom and so that your glory might be reflected and magnified throughout the world. **Amen.**

PROPER 29: CHRIST THE KING *Sunday Closest to November 23*

Glorious God, in confidence and hope we lift our needs and hopes to you in anticipation of your response as we say, Lord in your mercy, hear our prayer.

Clothe your church with humility and grace, that the sacrificial love of Jesus may course through every mission, every ministry, every program, and every faithful servant.
Lord in your mercy, **hear our prayer.**

Help our nation to use wisely the blessings of our history, our geography, our industry, our culture, and our people, so that we might find common purpose and meaning in ensuring the well-being of all who call this land home.
Lord in your mercy, **hear our prayer.**

Move through every heart of this assembly and open us up to the possibilities of your love and excite us for the sake of your ministry.
Lord in your mercy, **hear our prayer.**

You have placed Christ over all Creation, help us to ensure that the goodness with which it was formed might be preserved and sustained that he might reign over a plentiful and beautiful earth.
Lord in your mercy, **hear our prayer.**

Christ knew suffering on the cross, may He be present with those who are suffering now and walk with them into the peace and wholeness of his ever-present love.
Lord in your mercy, **hear our prayer.**

Relieve us from the fear of death and grant us entrance into God's glorious eternal presence when our mortal journey has ended.
Lord in your mercy, **hear our prayer.**

You may have made Christ our Lord and His name is the name at which every knee shall bow, yet even in his glory he is grace, humility, and love. Help us to walk his path and be his faithful servants, through the same Christ who abides with you and the Holy Spirit, now and always. **Amen.**

www.ingramcontent.com/pod-product-compliance
Ingram Content Group UK Ltd.
Pitfield, Milton Keynes, MK11 3LW, UK
UKHW021833140426
5217IPUK00021B/1425